Faith in Children

Dedicated to Gordon, Claire, and James,
who have each taught me so much.

Faith
in Children

Ronni Lamont

MONARCH
BOOKS

Published by
Lion Hudson Limited
Wilkinson House, Jordan Hill Business Park
Banbury Road, Oxford OX2 8DR, England
www.lionhudson.com

ISBN 978 0 8572 1951 0
eISBN 978 0 8572 1952 7

First edition 2020

Acknowledgments
Scripture quotations marked NRSV are from The New Revised Standard Version of the Bible Copyright © 1989 by the Division of Christian Education of the National Council of Churches in the USA. Used by permission. All Rights Reserved. The author has added italics to Scripture quotations for emphasis.

p.90 image of Growth tree © Sarah Brush.

A catalogue record for this book is available from the British Library

Printed and bound in the UK, March 2020, LH26

Contents

Introduction

Twelve years ago, I wrote the introduction to *Understanding Children Understanding God*.[1] The years since have been full of huge changes in the world of children's spirituality as well as my own personal life. The field has rapidly grown, as has my own understanding and knowledge, and so we come to a new revised version of the book.

As I have moved publishers, home, and working pattern, this new book has a new title which reflects some of the changes of the past decade or so. But I have kept the bare bones of many chapters, and this introduction, as well as including new thinking and theory which I have come across and enjoyed using over the years – and I hope you do too. So we need to go back in time, for the Sophie who features in this introductory story is now a young adult…

It was my week to tell the story in Sunday school.[2] I told the story, we sang some songs and said a prayer, and I went into church, to do my bit for the rest of the congregation. Later on, Sophie (six), came up to me.

"Ronni, you've got very big black boots."

"Yes, Sophie, that's because I've got big feet."

"God must have enormous boots, Ronni."

I think I replied something like, "Yes, God must have enormous boots, mustn't he, Sophie?"

Children say things that adults do not. It's partly social conditioning, partly self-consciousness and not wanting to look foolish, but it's also because children think differently from adults. St Paul was right when he said, "When I was a child, I spoke like a child, I thought like a child, I reasoned like a child; when I became an adult, I put an end to childish ways" (1 Corinthians 13:11).

As children grow up, their thinking processes change, so they stop thinking childish thoughts.[3] The premise of this book is that we should value what children say in their childish ways as it opens back up to adults the child's rightly childish view of God. Deep within us all is the child who thought in childish ways and spoke in childish ways; the way of thinking, speaking, and being before self-consciousness strikes, and we become tongue tied and less able to share our innate spirituality.

Without listening to our children, we cannot recapture that very different way of doing theology, which many in our culture perceive as somehow "less" than an adult's way of doing theology.

Jerome W. Berryman, in his introductory book entitled *Godly Play*,[4] states his clearly held belief that children are born with knowledge of God, and that this is as natural to them as breathing. It is as we grow up that we lose that innate belief as we ask the inevitable questions of our childish belief and take on the values of the largely secular world around us. Our awareness of the world overpowers this spirituality and we lose that knowledge of God with us, even if we did not have the name for God.

Jesus told us that unless we become as children we cannot enter the kingdom of heaven. There have been many interpretations of that radical statement. This book explores a child's spirituality and view of God and the kingdom of heaven, hoping that by understanding children, we adults will be helped to understand God. By understanding a child's faith, we are enabled to understand ourselves in a deeper manner.

The first chapters of the book give an overview of the various theories that have been developing over the last 100 years; tools to help us understand the children that we work with. Please don't be tempted to skip over these chapters – they are critical if we are to understand where Sophie's comment came from. These tools help us to re-enter that place where we have once been and now find it so hard to return. The place where God is so present for many of our children.

The later chapters of the book contain some practical ideas and strategies on how, I believe, we can work with and learn from our children as we journey together in our lives of faith.

This book was originally written for my own Sunday school teachers, back when I was a vicar, as I realized they didn't have the knowledge of child development that would complement their love and enthusiasm for working with children, and that would inform them and enable their ministries to flourish. As time has gone by, I realize that many in other ministries have found this knowledge helpful, so it has become a book for anyone who is in ministry with any age.

At the end of each chapter there are a few questions, for groups of those who minister with children to ponder together, perhaps at planning meetings. They could also be used in ministry teams of many types, as together we share the kingdom of God in all its richness.

CHAPTER 1

Spirituality

God means good to me. And my family. The best thing is God. When I am lonely, I think of God and I feel better.
Marayyam, eight years old

What do I mean when I use the word "spirituality"? What do you mean when you use the word? Spirituality is a vague word, one that is commonly heard, but not often in the same sentence as "church, worship, congregation, Sunday school..." Today's concept of spirituality is exceptionally slippery, and very subjective to the person using the word. With the rise in mindfulness, meditation, and other spiritual practices, many people now describe themselves as "spiritual but not religious" and therein may lie the nub of the matter.

My computer's thesaurus defines "spirituality" as, "Religion, theology, religious studies, mysticism, holiness."

The aim of this chapter is to examine what the word spirituality means to me, and therefore to help you to examine what it might mean for you. We will then move on to looking at what it might mean within the confines of this book.

A good way into this discussion is through that common comment above, "I am spiritual but not religious." Let's look at a typical person espousing that view: Thirty years ago, she was religious. She now worships at the Society of Friends (Quakers) yet does not describe herself as a religious person. What does this mean? Many people would agree, describing themselves as spiritual but towards the agnostic/atheistic end of the "belief in God" spectrum.

Try this for yourself: Ask people what they think the word "spirituality" means. They will probably reply using words such as "love, peace, inner self, hope, tranquillity." They may mention religious belief, as my thesaurus did, but if they live outside of organized religion it will come later in their personal list.

Now ask them what "religion" means. They'll probably use words such as "church, funeral, marriages, baptism, Christmas, Easter, Christians, Muslims, and so on." The two lists do not have many common words, but the tone is different; the list to do with "spirituality" feels more positive, more desirable in this day and age. "Religion" comes across as a more negative concept, more to do with "Thou shalt not" than "Thou shalt." One is very personal, the second much more to do with society and our institutions. One is full of the desirables of a full and inclusive, holistically healthy life, the other of optional add-ons for those who require such things. Religion can sometimes cause as many problems as it gives answers. Spirituality is thought of as an opening up, a third dimension to life, and one that most people are very positive about. Religion; well, that depends on what this week's headlines are as to how positively people respond to the word and all the baggage it brings with it. The necessary structures within religion are now thought of by many in the population as controlling and unhelpful, while spirituality is liberating and seen to be advantageous in one's personal inner journey.

In the book *The Spirit of the Child*,[1] the relationship between spirituality and religion is modelled as a tree, where the roots are a person's spirituality and the leaves are their religion. Thus, the spirituality is the deep down, unseen part of the person's faith life, and the leaves, so conspicuous and clear, mark them out as religious. The metaphor could be taken to extremes – perhaps Anglicans are oak trees, Roman Catholics sycamores, Muslims... And the last comment to make before the metaphor is taken to ridiculous extremes is that while the leaves may indeed fall off a tree, it's only dead when the roots die. So it is that people may well be spiritual without any trappings of religious belief or conviction. These people may only go to church or a place of worship to mark the important rites of passage for their family, or others, such as weddings or funerals. They may be one of the millions who regularly attend church at Christmas and Easter, but not usually in between. They may be one of the millions who went regularly as a child but stopped when something else was more important on a Sunday. Or they may be one of the many people who like to enter churches when they are empty, to think and commune with their inner being without any overt guidance as to how that process should be undertaken. I would encourage all who are reading this book to notice the spirituality that flows through all human beings, or at least has the potential to be there within each of us. And this applies to children especially.

This common potential spirituality was brought to our attention in particular through the work of Alister Hardy, who, as retired Professor of Zoology at Oxford University gave the Gifford Lectures at the University of Aberdeen in 1965. In these lectures, Hardy, a committed Darwinist, stated that he believed that religious experience has evolved through the process of natural selection; that being religious in some way gave *Homo sapiens* an evolutionary edge. Religiosity was of survival value to the individual. He was saying that there is a form of awareness that is over and above our "normal" awareness of what is going on around us, which transcends that everyday awareness. This special awareness is potentially present in all human beings and has a positive function in our lives, enabling us to survive, and that the many religions that are present in our world are the natural outworkings of that transcendent awareness. The religions of the world vary according to the culture in which they arise, taking local cultural norms and refining the religion to reflect and reinforce those particular norms. He also believed that religious awareness is an expression of a psychological predisposition or a process that is present for all of us, and that there is a section of the brain that has evolved to undertake this awareness. The awareness is not "owned" by any one religion, but those religions show that it is indeed common, right across the globe, in all cultures. It is even seen in people who are alienated from religious culture, and this may be an important observation in our increasingly secular society. Thus religious awareness is thought to be potentially present in all of us.

There are various theories as to how this spiritual awareness became the religions that we now see around us in the world: Religion may come from ancient philosophies, with traditional philosophy underpinning the particular form of faith. Or it may be that it is an outworking of a common experience, a spiritual awareness that is common to humanity. Or it could be that religious experience is coming out of a culture, and entering a religion means that you have to become competent in the language of that particular religion. It could be a combination of these three theories, but the last one means that if anyone is to comprehend and grow in their chosen religion, it is imperative that they have the language to negotiate that faith. How could anyone be a Christian without hearing the word "sin" and understanding what that tiny but powerful little word means?[2] Yet we assume that when we say "sin", everyone listening knows what that means. The same is true for all the language that is used within the context of the church and its workings. Religious language is a clear form of jargon (a specific set of words and concepts necessary to an area of understanding), and if we do not ensure that those who are joining our faith are not clearly helped to understand the vocabulary of our faith, they will not be able to access worship or any more than a very basic form of teaching. This is an important idea, and one that we will return to later.

So, across the globe, this awareness gave rise to religions. It is this awareness that many people define as "spirituality". Lectures on spirituality at the Alister Hardy Religious Experience Research Centre at Oxford University (now at the University of Wales) were followed by work by David Hay at Nottingham University. Hay has since published his research investigating the common spiritual experiences of human beings in the UK in such books as *Religious Experience Today* (Mowbray, 1990).

At least 50 per cent of the population will acknowledge having had such an experience, many in childhood, many when the person was alone.[3] The experiences are often spoken about as sensing a presence, of the person knowing that the presence was good and loving. In a recent conversation, I heard the story of how, after giving birth, a woman was left on her own, and she saw a beautiful blue-white light in the room. She knew that this was God and that great goodness was emanating from the light. To this day, she still puzzles over the "why?"

It is worth noting that people who are not able to access a good quality of life, who are oppressed and unable to articulate well, will be less likely to speak of a religious experience, and that there is a significant association between having a spiritually rich inner life with good health and personal happiness.[4]

There are suggestions in the research that spirituality is more evidently present in children than in adults. This may be due to the pattern of Western culture where there is an expectation that we keep our religious experiences to ourselves (and if you do speak of your spiritual life, it's like taking a cork out of a bottle in my experience) and so our spirituality is an internal affair, little discussed and not related to the mainstream consciousness around us. As children grow up, they recognize that adults don't speak of or share their spiritual lives, and so neither will the children. Sadly, this means that many adults don't even have the language needed to share their spiritual life, should they wish so to do.[5] One of our tasks as ministers is to share with children and adults the language with which they can articulate and explore their spiritual lives, be they inside or outside of a religious context.

Children and spirituality

Heaven lies about us in our infancy!
Shades of the prison-house begin to close
Upon the growing boy,
But he beholds the light, and whence it flows,
He sees it in his joy;
The youth, who daily farther from the east
Must travel, still is nature's Priest

And by the vision splendid
Is on his way attended;
At length the man perceives it die away,
And fade into the light of common day.[6]

Within the above lines, there is a profound realization that children have a glimpse of heaven within their souls that is lost as they mature, that they find thinking about spirituality far easier than adults, and that their ability to be in touch with themselves at this profound level is lost as they "mature".

There is an apocryphal story about Coleridge: When he came across a woman with a newborn baby, he picked up the baby and sternly asked the child, "Tell me, tell me what it was like…"

I once read that the eyes of a newborn child are unfocused as the child's soul hasn't quite arrived yet, and that their look is direct from heaven.[7] This relates to Augustine's theory that we revisit in the prayer, "O God, our hearts are restless until they find their rest in you," referring to his (still orthodox) belief that all souls are present with God in heaven before they join their human shape, and then return to God in heaven when that human shape has expired.

So what happens to our children's easy spirituality? There is no doubt that as they grow up they absorb far more about life from the modelling that they experience from those around them than from their words.[8] I may tell my children to share their insights about God and the world, but if I don't share my experiences and ideas with them as easily as they share theirs with mine, they are going to notice, very quickly, that this isn't an area of conversation that adults easily enter. What goes on at home, even in an open home where such discussions are welcomed, is not mirrored in life, so the children will hold onto their insights, perhaps sharing them at home or at church, and then, eventually, probably not sharing them at all. This is one of the benefits of a church school; children hear belief in God and spiritual awareness as normal throughout the day, and so their spiritual flourishing can be facilitated. What happens when they go up to secondary school, which is far less likely to be a church school, is well acknowledged as their faith gets lost in the pressure of non-religious peers, and the onslaught of hormones and adolescence. If they don't talk about their spirituality, they won't grow in their use of more sophisticated language to help them to understand increasingly sophisticated spiritual/religious concepts, and so their reasoning stalls and stops.

It is clear that the way forward is to attentively listen to what children have to say, and so draw alongside the child, imagining as much of their inner life as we can, and then go there to help them. This is, of course, easier said than done. When my thinking is that of an adult, and theirs is that of a child (see chapter 2 on Cognitive Development for a clearer understanding of the difference) this can feel like running up a slope, but this is what we need to do. And, like running up that slope, it gets easier with practice. With practice, you will find once again the child that is within you and has always been – and that child will value your attention and love.

Children's spiritual awareness is revealed in many ways.[9] Firstly, they are very aware; they can "feel" a mood and are easily taken there by music or by looking at pictures. Light a candle and let a child hold it and watch the rapture on their faces as they look into the flame. Like many clergy, as a vicar I resisted Christingle services on grounds of "health and safety", but I changed my attitude towards the service when an adult told me how much it meant to her as a child – it was one of her key moments in her growth in faith as a Christian. Children can focus in on the mood and dwell in the moment far better than most adults. This is partly because, unlike me, they're not wondering what to cook for supper, or where that top came from that someone's wearing, whether I turned on the burglar alarm as I left the house. If we can leave all our external fretting behind, we too can enter into the magic of the child's concentration on a simple candle flame, a flock of birds, a newborn lamb, or even of a plane taking off. Children will be excited by many things that adults ignore simply because we're so used to them, and if we can go there with them, our world will open up and become the sparkling place that children occupy in these moments. This period of a child's life is not eternal – at the point where language and symbols begin to merge in the mind, the child loses the ability to just "be" as they try to behave in a more "adult" manner. Enjoy it while you can!

Because children are sensitive and are easily taken into a mood, we need to ensure we are not manipulating them to a place where we can push them towards something that they may otherwise not agree to. I have been at events where children are urged to respond to an altar call to commit their lives to Christ. Whilst it may seem very successful, the children are more likely to have been responding to the adult (probably unconsciously) manipulating the mood of the event, or from children's love of being in with the others and following the crowd. Because of this, in my opinion, I do not think that altar calls are appropriate for children.

Children have a great sense of awe. They will stop at the brow of a hill and just look, taking in the vista. When the children from the local school come to look round my church, the ones who have never been in before often stop in the doorway with their jaws open: "What an enormous place, so high, so beautiful," they seem to be thinking. The building itself, designed by the Victorians to inspire awe, was achieving that aim in these children. I remember as a child going to (a modern) church for choir practice one evening. There were no adults there so we "dared" each other to touch the altar table. I was terrified, and quite expected a bolt of lightning to send me on my way. It didn't, but I can still remember the feeling of intruding into a "holy space" where I felt I had no right to be. Saying the words of the prayer of consecration after being ordained was similar. What was I doing, saying these words? It was surely someone's else's role, not mine. In my last parish, while going through a preparation course for our children to receive Communion prior to being confirmed (see chapter 13), we asked the children to go and sit somewhere that they felt was holy, where they could feel close to God. Two shared my seat (in the chancel area, behind a screen). Two went up and sat by the altar. Another sat on the organist's seat, another couple up in the pulpit, others around the chancel, inside the "holy" area defined by the screen that extends across the church. They had a very clear sense of where the holy part of the church was and entered that area with some trepidation the first time.

We see children's spirituality through their use of the imagination. Read through some of the comments from children that are included in this book – they are stunningly imaginative about God, God's life, and his activity in the world.

> *I think God is my best friend. He makes me happy when I'm sad and I think of him when I am lonely. When I close my eyes we sing songs to each other. I love it.*
>
> **Ruby, eight years old**

Anyone who works with children will have such examples to give of how children experience God in the imagination as they go through life. For me, it is one of the greatest joys of working with children.

Children understand that God is good, and they understand that in a quite sophisticated way. They seek God when unhappy, expecting God to come close and cheer them up, providing company when lonely, and even someone to sing with!

Many adults will be familiar with the experience of music taking you out of yourself, to a "higher plane". This is familiar too for children, who will listen intently to music, clearly "miles away" in their enjoyment. Similarly, a walk through woods or the local park may give a similar raised awareness in any of us, and children are particularly open to this, watching birds and animals with more patience than many adults.

You may also be familiar with the feeling of not thinking about something that you do well, that is effortless. My best experiences of this have been when dancing, or galloping on a horse that knows exactly at which point it should slow down because you're nearing the end of the gallop. This is called "flow" and is common to most people. Ask them what they were thinking about at that point and they may give you a puzzled look – they are just there, in the moment.

Adults will feel very grateful for these spiritual moments breaking into their lives, while children seem to have a more seamless join between their spiritual and physical experiences. Rebecca Nye has coined a name for these experiences, when we would just like to hold on to a special moment that we are sharing with a child, when Christians might say something of God breaks in, and we pause. She calls it a MOG[10] – a Moment of Ordinary Grace. And the frustrating thing is that it is completely non-quantifiable. You can't even ask the child if they're aware of it, as they would just look puzzled and the moment will have been wrecked. Talk to anyone who works with children, and MOGs are what keeps them doing it – an extraordinary moment when a child makes you aware of how close they are to God at that point in time.

You may be thinking that I'm now beginning to describe the better religious rituals that you have been to; indeed, the theory is that our worship should indeed take people to a place where they let go of their consciousness and just "go with the flow". Thus our awareness of the spiritual is heightened, for adults as well as for children. You may also be thinking that some of the experiences I've described are not what you would usually call "spiritual". Perhaps one of the tasks of this book is to encourage religious folk to let the world share a concept that we have for many years felt was our own private affair.

Spirituality is all around us and within us. We have briefly considered how it is integrated into each individual, and in the next few chapters we move on to consider how children develop in various ways, giving the multifaceted individuals that we are all becoming, and where spirituality is to be found in that blend.

Questions for discussion

1. What do you mean by "spirituality"? Perhaps write up your group's comments on a flipchart and see if you can reach a common mind or a definition for your place of worship.

2. Do you agree that people can be spiritual without being religious? If not, can you say what is resisting this idea within you?

3. What words found within your worship do you find it difficult to explain to children? Or to adults?

4. Can you share any religious acts, or services, which you found particularly meaningful for you? Would you be prepared to share these with the group?

5. What other experiences in life would you now describe as spiritual?

CHAPTER 2

Psychological theories of childhood: intellectual development

As a curate in 1959 I was taking a class of 5/6 year olds (St Peter Chorley, Diocese of Blackburn). During the subject "saints" near the end of the lesson we had a list of 200 saints names on the blackboard, then the bell sounded for the mid-morning break. Everyone left except a little girl, Jean. "What is the matter," I asked? "We have missed one out," she said. "Who?" I asked. "Saint Freddie," came her reply. "Do you know about St Freddie?" I asked. "Oh yes," came the reply. "Do tell me," I said. This was her reply: "Well, you see curate, when I was four my mum had a little baby and we called him Freddie, but when he was ten days old he died." "Oh, I am sorry," I interjected. "Oh, it's alright," she continued, "cos you see curate, if a saint is somebody who never did or said anything wrong to anybody, then we have a saint in our family and his name is Freddie." We wrote the name "St Freddie" on the blackboard and off she went skipping into the playground to join her friends.

George Dewhurst, personal correspondence, 2007

Just how do children's minds develop as they grow older? A baby is so different from a toddler, who is so different from a primary-aged child, who is so different from an adolescent, who is so different from an adult. This chapter looks at the theories of how this amazing process takes place and how we see intellectual development through the ways and being of a child.

Intellectual development

There are three views held at the moment amongst psychologists about a child's intellectual development.

There is the **psychometric**, based in measuring a child's intelligence, giving scores such as IQ. However, this does not include the perceptible fact that as children grow older their thinking changes and becomes more abstract.

This led to a second view, **cognitive development**, which focuses on structures rather than intellectual power. It looks at how children are changing the way they handle new information or data, and the common traits of thinking that all children display rather than looking at how clever each child is.

Today, these two models have been partially integrated to give the **information processing approach**, which regards intelligence not as a faculty or trait of the mind, but that intelligence is about processing.

There is little to say about psychometric theories other than exams like the 11+ are often still based upon them. You can indeed measure a person's IQ, and while that will tell you how intelligent they are, it is a very one-dimensional snapshot of that person at a moment in time. Ironically, it does not discriminate between which subject areas the person is good at. My son at thirteen had quite a high IQ but was average (by the school's definition) at maths. This was confusing for the grammar school we were hoping he would attend following a house move… he didn't study maths at university either.

IQ tests continue to be used, but most organizations that test people will use a more wide-ranging form of psychometric testing. Hopefully we no longer value people just for their IQ, but that's another story.

When I went to teacher training college, many years ago, I learnt about the theory of cognitive intelligence development, as put forward by Jean Piaget. One of our lecturers, whom we liked to impersonate, had a favourite saying: "Trying to understand Piaget is like trying to start a car on a cold morning." At that time, we were taught Piaget rather as if he was the gospel truth; now there has been time for developments and more research Piaget is less revered. But there is still value in looking at his theory – much of it will resonate within those of us who have watched children at play or at work.

Jean Piaget (1896-1980) looked at the form and structure of children's thinking as they develop over the years. He asked the questions, "How do children understand the world around them?" and "What kind of logic are they using to help them comprehend the world in which they live, and how does that logic change as they grown older?"

He started with "How does a child's knowledge of the world develop?" by making the central assumption that the child is an active participant in the development of their internal knowledge – that children reach out to the world to learn all about it and so take part in it. He thought that as children grow older they construct their own understanding of what is happening to them and within them.

This means that everyone thinks differently, and that is so important for us all to take on board. Every single person's brain works differently, and children are very different from adults, in ways that we will be examining later in this chapter. But if this idea is new to you, take a pause to process it; this is why some children and people are just so exasperating – they think very differently to you. And if you're finding my style of writing annoying, perplexing, or invigorating, that tells you how similar (or not!) my thinking is to yours. (We will explore this again when we look at other aspects of our personalities, and especially in the chapter on Spiritual Styles.)

The modern metaphor favoured for this theory is that of the "little scientist"; someone who is actively exploring the world, seeking understanding and knowledge. Think about a crawling baby – they scour their world, picking up whatever takes their eye, and usually putting it into their mouth, the best sense receptor of a small person. If it's not removed by a hovering carer, the child will taste and roll the object around, trying out its surfaces and texture. How does the child know the difference between mashed banana and mashed dirt otherwise? The older child will gaze at new objects, turn them over in their hands, possibly lick them (how efficient was that carer?) and if the right things are to hand, may well measure or draw them. If I find something new, I will look at it carefully before picking it up, in case it should be something harmful. Many years ago, walking in the Lake District, my husband and I came across a (live) snake on the path. I proceeded to pick it up while he endeavoured not to panic. I was a biology teacher at the time, and what was critical was not that I recognized the snake, more that I picked it up correctly, holding it just behind the head. (It was a grass snake.) I was using information that I had internalized at some point in my life. My husband was not party to that information, but is now! At about the same time, I was head of year at a comprehensive school, in charge of what would now be called year 9 students. I had a super batch of cheeky special needs lads, who liked practical jokes. One day, I found a dead mouse on my desk in my office. Not being at all squeamish I picked up the dead mouse, took it to the special needs room, and put it on one of these lad's desks. He thought it was hilarious and had more respect for me afterwards. He had expected me to act as many people would – to create a huge fuss over a dead mouse. He learned that I wasn't squeamish and also enjoyed a joke.

Piaget thought that a child tries to adapt to the world that it lives in, and as the child gets older they do it in increasingly successful ways. The process of adaptation takes time, and is made up of several sub processes, and here we must use some jargon:

A **scheme** is roughly the same as the word **concept** – a mental category or complex of ideas. So if you say the word "dog" to me, I have a clear mental picture, a concept, of what the word "dog" represents. In my last parish, I had a dog who clearly was a very doggy dog – lots of children wanted to stroke him, and tiny children said "dog" or "woof" when they saw him. Actually, I think he looked more like a Jacob sheep with a dog's head, but that's a matter of perspective and my confused scheme regarding sheep and shaggy dogs. If you were to say "black Labrador" then I have an even clearer picture of what you are talking about – I have a concept of dog, which includes black Labradors. My dog is not part of the black Labrador scheme, and never will be.

Piaget takes this a bit further, saying that knowledge is not a passive mental category, but comprises actions, either mental or physical, and each of these actions is a scheme. The scheme is not actually the categorization, but the action of categorizing. When the child looked at my dog, she was using her looking scheme. When she reached out and grabbed a fistful of his lovely woolly coat, she was using her grasping scheme. Babies have a limited repertoire of schemes, but, as you can surmise, this repertoire is added to at an amazing rate and grows very quickly. The crawling toddler knows something by its feel, look, and taste. Two years later that same toddler will use very different methods to judge an object.

The word that is used for this intake of knowledge is **assimilation**. Children assimilate information and incorporate it into their thinking, their schemes. The small toddler that first saw my dog heard an adult say "dog" as she reached out. "Doggies say woof" may also be there in her environment. So next time, when she is beginning to speak and she sees something like my dog, she'll reach out and say "dog" or "woof". She has assimilated my dog as "dog". She may well realize that not all dogs look the same, but there is something she is picking up on – four legs, tail, certain shape head, droopy tongue – that sparks "dog" internally. Assimilation is an active process and we select the information that we assimilate. Colour is in particular subjective – if you ask my husband about a particular set of glasses and matching water jug that we have, he'd say that they are green. I'd say that they are brown. Who can say what colour they really are? But for him, the colour they are had been assimilated into his "shades of green" scheme, while for me, they are in my "shades of brown" scheme. We are both right, and both wrong. If only all arguments were so easily solved.

It may be that for my dog to enter a child's "dog" scheme, she has to adjust and alter the boundary of "dog" to include four-legged animals with a tail and the right shaped head, to include those with a woolly coat. If this is done, then she has **accommodated** her scheme – changed it to include new information about the attributes of that scheme. Shaggy dogs and short-haired dogs are both still "dog". Accommodation is the key to developmental change: It's how we re-organize our thoughts to take in new skills and change our strategies. It's how our concepts grow and develop, a widening of our thinking, to let new information interplay with what we already have to create something new, but recognizable as having grown out of what was there before.

As children learn and develop, they are always working to keep a balance, to keep a world view that makes sense. New data may be accommodated, and the scheme grows and develops. But if something comes along which changes the whole thing, then the original scheme may have to be ditched and restarted. It is much like a scientist working on a theory; they will try different experiments to test the theory. Some data will back up the theory, some will speak against it. Eventually, either the old theory has been effectively proven, or a new one forms to replace it. The critical thing is internal cohesion. Thus the child comes to a point of **equilibrium**, a balance that makes sense. At some point the child will learn that my dog was not a sheep – no matter how profound the resemblance! – and, more importantly, that sheep are not dogs. On my first day as a teacher, I only learnt the basic route around school – how to find the rooms I needed; science block, staff room, toilets. As I spent more time in the school, I learned more details – where the kids smoked, where the teachers smoked, where the Head's study was. I learned which corridors had locked doors at the end, and to which I didn't have a key, and so I retraced my steps to find a real thoroughfare. In learning the geography of the school, the times I made mental corrections, I was accommodating, and the times I decided I was lost, mentally scrubbed the map and started again, were my striving for equilibrium.

Piaget thought that a child operated in a similar way, to create coherent, fairly consistent models or theories to live by. However, babies inevitably start with a limited repertoire of schemes, and new data coming up against these inadequacies in those schemes force a major upheaval every now and then as the baby becomes a child, and so on. Piaget found that these radical reworkings seemed to occur at about the same age in the children that he studied.

He saw three major points of change:

The **first is at about eighteen months**. Here there seems to be a shift from the dominance of simple sensory and motor schemes to a child beginning to use the first symbols. This is also the age at which children begin to speak coherently.

The **second is between the ages of five and seven**, when the child adds a new set of powerful schemes which Piaget called **operations**. The child can suddenly understand far more complicated and general mental actions, such as mental arithmetic.

The **third takes place at adolescence**, when the child works out how to "operate on" ideas as well as objects – the beginning of abstract thought.

Piaget thus gives us four stages:

- **Sensorimotor**, from birth to eighteen months.

- **Preoperational**, from eighteen months to about five years.

- **Concrete operations**, from about five years to twelve.

- **Formal operations**, from twelve upwards.

Here you may be thinking, "Gosh, that sort of reflects our school ages." Something was being recognized long before Piaget gave us his theory.

Let's look at these stages in a little more detail.

Sensorimotor

This stage is involved with making sense of the world into which our child has been born. The child assimilates information to the limited array of sensory and motor schemes that she was born with. Looking and listening, grasping and sucking, she works to accommodate schemes that come to her through her senses and motor abilities. This age is the starting point for all cognitive development, and the child lives entirely in the present. She responds to the stimuli that come at her, but does not remember, or plan, or intend. As she goes through life, she will begin to change, until she knows that her mother or primary carer will always be the same person (unless dire events have taken place) and her doll or teddy is always the same object. Daddy has a deeper voice and dirt isn't as nice to eat as banana, although it gets a much bigger response from mummy or daddy. She's not able to manipulate these images or use symbols to stand for them. When the ability to manipulate her internal symbols begins to take place it shows that she has reached the next stage. It's been said, rather unflatteringly (towards the child!), that the thinking of a child at this stage can be likened to that of a dog. It's a form of non-contemplative intelligence. As parents will know, development during this stage can be very fast indeed, often seeming to be in leaps rather than gradual growth.

Research, however, has shown that Piaget may not be totally correct in that there is now evidence that babies do remember from very early days. They learn how to hold a rattle, and who their carer is very quickly, and they remember that person – whether it is shape, voice, smell, or a combination. Certainly, modern psychologists think babies are far more sophisticated than Piaget gave them credit. Critically, all agree that over the second half of a child's second year, the thinking shifts and moves into symbolic thoughts. This coincides with a child beginning to use language as their primary means of communication and is reflected in the onset of tantrums. It must be said that it is, of course, very difficult to research young babies as you can only observe – you can't engage them in a dialogue to check out what you have seen, or what you think you've seen. This only comes with the next stage.

Preoperational

This is a delightful stage, when the child isn't having a "wobbly". He is using symbols in his thinking, and imagination and creativity are rampant in his play. Children in this stage can turn a cardboard box into a house, a car, a tank. Piles of bricks reach up towards the ceiling, hideouts are made under the table. A playhouse can see the child inside for hours on end. Children take on roles in their playing – mummies and daddies – although the children find it very hard to play in role with others if they don't all want the same outcomes! The child has rigid thinking; "This is what mummies do" will only reflect what that child's mummy does, not a general "mummy". A child at this age thinks that everyone sees the world exactly as they do – hence the tantrums when it seems that everyone doesn't. The classic Piaget observation at this age is if you pour identical amounts of fruit juice into a short, fat glass and into a tall, thin one, the child just knows that the tall, thin one contains more. You could pour the contents of the tall, thin glass into a short, fat one, and they would still insist that the tall, thin one held more juice. (If you've never observed this, try it! It's quite stunning for an adult to watch this taking place – you simply cannot convince the child that the amount really is the same.) This is the principle of conservation, and it's a concept that children of this age just can't handle. Likewise, if you show a child a picture of a glass of water and then draw the outline of a glass on its side and ask the child to draw in the water, they will draw a line at 90 degrees to the glass – they don't realise that the water will have come out. This sounds so weird to adults, but it certainly took my son a long time, and lots of wet tablecloths, to recognize how liquids spill.

New research implies that children in this stage are less egotistic than Piaget suggested, but they do indeed struggle with appearance and reality. They cannot predict the actions of others just from observation. Children of this age don't understand that "you know that I know" or that people are thinking all the time, although they recognize that everyone thinks. This doesn't come until they are moving into the next stage, and this reciprocal thinking is needed for real friendship.

Children in this stage understand that there is a link between emotions and circumstances; "My dog died, so I'm sad." They are learning the social rules about self-expression – that throwing a tantrum in Tesco's (or anywhere else) is not acceptable. That it's appropriate to smile if things are going well or funny, but not if someone is sad. The "social smile" comes at about three, although very small children may have a reflex smile for a camera. Language during this stage is growing increasingly sophisticated, and once it achieves a certain level, using vocabulary such as "want", "need", "think" and "remember", the child will enter the next stage.

Concrete operations

The child has by now discovered or developed a set of abstract rules or strategies for examining and interacting with the world around them, and these are the concrete operations referred to. An operation for Piaget is a set of powerful, abstract, internal schemes, many associated with mathematical thinking – addition, multiplication, division, ordering, and so on. They are the building blocks of logical thinking, giving the child internal rules about objects and the way that they relate – three is always less than four. Houses are more than one storey high, adding gives a bigger number, subtraction a smaller one. They can look at a page of sums and have a crucial understanding of what the answers should look like. The child will now understand that dogs come in different shapes and sizes, and while a Labrador is always a dog, dogs aren't always Labradors. Children enjoy "hands-on" learning experiences, and are able to go from this particular experience, "Look at this river valley, what do we notice," to the general, "So are all river valleys like this?" Children of this age love to count species and enjoy cataloguing. They can't yet handle deductive logic, where you start with a principle and work towards an outcome or an observation, as they cannot imagine what they haven't seen or experienced. The reason this stage is called concrete operations is that the child is working with the concrete – what they can see in front of them. They will enjoy becoming knowledgeable about certain subjects, a classic example being dinosaurs, football, or the latest band, and can tell you all about these things in great depth. They will learn new information about these things very easily – as do we all. Expertise makes a big difference at all ages, and this is the stage where it begins.

Formal operations

Children experience enormous changes as they enter adolescence, and this age varies enormously from child to child. However, by about twelve, children will be entering the next stage, that of formal operations. Here, thinking begins to shift, from the concrete to the abstract. What is possible can now be imagined and thought through. The child can now extend their concrete operations and reasoning to include objects or situations that she has not experienced directly. Teenagers plan their wardrobes without actually being in the cupboard with their clothes. They spend a lot of time thinking about their future life – falling in love, long-term relationships, work and career paths. The most obvious effect for many is the self-consciousness that is typical; suddenly young people are aware of being and being observed; "I know that you know that I know," "I'm aware of you being aware that I'm aware of you." The permutations are endless!

They are now able to systematically solve problems. Algebra appears in the maths curriculum, chemistry involves scientific equations involving atoms and molecules that the children probably will never actually see at all but understand and turn around in their minds.

At one time I found myself teaching secondary science and frequently heard myself say to children who just couldn't grasp such equations, 'Don't worry, it will come, it will all fall into place one day soon.' And indeed, most times it did – the child would suddenly beam as the penny dropped and it all made sense.

Younger children use inductive logic, based on lots of individual experience and interaction. Older children use deductive logic, thinking "if this, then that…" and this kind of thinking is used in many branches of science, which, although taught at primary schools, makes a very different impression and is hugely developed at secondary school. During those first few years at secondary school, a child develops and changes rapidly, both physically, emotionally, and mentally. They learn to adapt theories and change what they know and believe to be true or correct, and so they become adults rather than children.

Formal operations demand a different level of thinking processes, and it has been estimated that only about 50-60 per cent of twenty-year-olds use this style of thinking in an industrialized nation such as Britain. The more heavily technological the society, the more need for formal operations. It could be that most of the time we simply don't need to be using formal operations – do I want to debate this over the dinner table or would I rather just chat? During most of my day-to-day life I am using concrete operations because that's all I need to use. Some adults never use formal operations – their thinking process never got there and so it has never been developed. This may be because they have limited IQ and do not have the mental ability to move into this style of thinking, or they have not been educated well enough to have that extensive vocabulary. Certainly, formal operations require an ability to juggle concepts mentally that not all achieve, and some form of language is at the root of that ability.

*　*　*

Critically, we all realize that children grow and develop in a continuous way, not in stages as Piaget's theory implies. The changes are usually gradual, and yet there are clear jumps in development that take place.

Piaget believed that development came through a child's interaction with objects. Lev Vygotsky (1896-1934), a Russian psychologist, believed that children are more affected by social interaction, saying that playing with others, be they adults or children, was more important than playing with things/toys. Evidence for this has come from a study where children growing up in larger families were found to be slightly more advanced in their thinking than only children in the way that they handled the concept of a false belief. This came about through the children learning about other people's feelings and reactions on a wider scale than children whose social interaction was limited within the family. Most educational psychologists now agree, and our social interaction with the children in our care is crucial for their development.

Understanding how our children grow and develop is critical if we are to target learning and support them as they do so. Whilst theories are only ever tools, we wouldn't try and dig the garden without a spade, neither would I recommend teaching and working with children without some idea of the processes and changes that are taking place inside the child as we watch, and frequently comment upon, the changes that are external.

Questions for discussion

1. What examples of children working in these different stages have you noticed?

2. How does your group help to expand the children's religious vocabulary as you work with them? How could this be improved?

3. How do you encourage your children to ask the difficult questions in an environment that is supportive?

CHAPTER 3

Personality development

Laura and her parents were walking out of church.
"Mummy, what's Jesus' first name?" asked Laura.
"What do you mean, Jesus' first name?" replied Laura's
mum.
"Well, God's called Peter, isn't he, so what's Jesus called?"
replied Laura.
"What do you mean, God's called Peter?" queried Laura's
mum.
"He's got to be called Peter. We say, 'Thanks Peter God',
don't we?" replied Laura.

Having spent time thinking about how a child develops intellectually, it may be worth thinking about how a child's personality develops. Personality is a difficult concept – what makes me me and you you? Why is everyone different, personality-wise, as well as in appearance? If we believe that every person is a gift of God, and made in God's image, then personality is a serious issue, and worth spending some time thinking over.

Personality is to do with the way that we all, children and adults, go about relating to the people and objects in the world around us. The differences that are there are enduring. I like horses, and always have done, you may not. Why do I like horses? Well, I could tell you why, but actually, I liked them before I could tell you why – I was just born like that... perhaps. You might like to spend a moment now thinking about the qualities that people have. Are they gregarious or shy, independent or dependent, are they a confident or uncertain person – you get the drift. Researchers refer to "the big five" personality traits: **extroversion, agreeableness, conscientiousness, neuroticism, and openness/intellect**.

Extroversion

Extroversion is perhaps the easiest to understand; it's the way in which someone engages with the world and social experiences. Extrovert people are gregarious and throw themselves into life. They tend to be active, assertive, enthusiastic, outgoing, and talkative. Introverts tend towards the opposite, taking time to adapt to new situations, being thoughtful and quiet. Interestingly, some people don't recognize themselves within this spectrum. A quick rule of thumb is that extroverts tend to speak before they think while introverts think before they speak. Extroverts gain energy from being with people, introverts from being on their own. One aspect of this to bear in mind when working with children and young people is the pressure that the present world puts upon them to be extrovert – even if they are not, which can lead introverted children to thinking there is "something wrong with them".[1] As Christians, we need to encourage all of those we come into contact with to be themselves, not some copy of what they might see around them, be it in real life or via social media, and that is increasingly hard. If we are working with a group of children or young people, it is critical that we allow time and space for introverts to join in with a discussion – be aware that extroverts will dominate and speak first, and you need to wait for introverts to join in slightly later on.

Agreeableness

Agreeableness is the extent to which a person's nature could be characterized by warmth and compassion, making up an affectionate, forgiving, and generous nature. The opposite is an antagonistic person, less trusting and sometimes tending to be unkind. An agreeable person may also be gullible and easily "conned".

Conscientiousness

Conscientiousness speaks of the extent and strength of a person's impulse control; how able are they to delay gratification, or does it have to be now? Conscientious people are efficient planners who are reliable, resourceful, and thorough in the way that they work and live.

Neuroticism

Neuroticism is about emotional stability; the extent to which the person experiences the world as worrying or distressing. Is the world a threatening place to be? Neurotic people tend to be touchy and irritable, tense and unstable.

Openness/intellect

Openness/intellect reflects the depth and complexity of a person's mental and experiential life. It includes how creative or artistic the person is, how imaginative they are, and how able they are to communicate that internal vision.

* * *

The question for us is how much of the above is true for children? How much develops later on in life as opposed to what we are born with, and how much develops rapidly as a response to the environment in which we are raised? Never forget the power of the child's immediate environment in the patterning of personality and the enduring way in which many adults treat boys and girls differently.

Certainly, these traits can be seen in older children and adolescents. Conscientiousness is the trait that is most clearly carried through – children who score highly on the conscientiousness trait tend to do well in school, but that's hardly surprising. Some psychologists would add two more traits: **irritability** and **activity**. These are self explanatory, and many younger children have high activity scores, and find it difficult to work at school "inside their head" rather than in an experiential manner.

Is temperament the same as personality? Temperament would

seem to be the substrate of personality, lying beneath the surface, and easily spotted if you dig in. The combination of the five traits would seem to be the mix from which the adult personality develops. But, as with adult personality, this is not fixed. Adults can work on their personality and develop aspects that they wish to, working on the shadow side, and so can children and young people.

Personality would seem to be the result of temperament being worked upon by the environment in which the child is growing. If a child is very active, moving a lot and frequently, there is a high chance that they will grow into an extrovert adult with a high sociability factor. There are also links between extroversion and agreeableness, but this could be because extroverts gain their acceptance from others rather than themselves internally.

Children who are inhibited as toddlers often grow into more shy children and adults. They may respond with fear or a withdrawal from new people or experiences, the opposite of the extrovert pattern of behaviour. These children may have higher scores on the neuroticism trait later in life. They may become angry, fussy, loud, or irritable as they go through school – the classic "difficult child". If skilled people can help them to control their difficulties and stay focused, managing their attention and effort, they will become more conscientious and grow more open to new experiences. Many schools work wonders with children who could be described as demanding and difficult when they arrive but learn through exposure to good practice to be more balanced and reflective individuals.

It is very important for us to realize that what is acceptable, normal; in one culture may not be so in another. A friend, who has a very active son, went to live in the USA when he was primary school age. Someone whom English teachers had seen as quite a demanding pupil, for he was also very bright, became a joy for American teachers working with children who were encouraged to be more expressive than English children typically are.

Research is indicating that a child's temperament will persist into adulthood as their personality. Babies who have a positive approach to the world tend to keep that positive outlook. Difficult babies tend to show that difficulty ten years later. Strongly inhibited babies tend to become shy adults.

The characteristics of a baby's temperament interact with the child's environment to either strengthen or modify that child. Parental response can make a huge difference to modifying a baby's temperament by their handling of the child. If parents are warm towards their child, the child will learn to be warm in the interaction with others too. If they are cold and distant, that will be the way that the child handles other people's approaches. If a shy child is encouraged to take part in the world and shown that they can indeed do that, then they will become less shy. If parents simply say, "Oh, she's shy" and leave the child to hide behind them, then the child may still be hiding behind their parent in the years to come.

Most children's temperaments fall within the midrange of the spectrum, and these children will adapt to their environments. Children with extreme temperaments will force their environment to adapt to them, so a difficult child will be told off more often and will have more negative reinforcement coming to them. They often have less support from their parents than a child who is less bother (but gain the attention that they may crave). Children with difficult temperaments are also likely to display emotional difficulties and difficult behaviour patterns. Sensitive parents can modify these more difficult patterns of behaviour to moderate it, but it is demanding work, as the glut of "nannying/parenting" programmes on the TV and the enormous amount of online debate, can show us. If behaviour is reinforced in a partial way, then the behaviour will probably get worse – that "naughty step", once decided on, must be carried through. "Lifting" strategies with children who are wakeful at night can often work amazingly quickly if the strategy is adhered to.[2]

Poor and inconsistent parental discipline for any child reaps problems later on in the child's life. It is even possible for parents to create a system at home where the children are actually in charge of the parents.

Twin studies indicate that some element of personality is inherited; studies carried out on twins growing up apart are well known. When twins who had never met were brought together, some were wearing identical clothes, had identical haircuts, and enjoyed the same activities. A Jewish friend once observed to me that God sends us the children we can least cope with – in that they remind us of ourselves! Certainly, the traits that I found most difficult in my children as small children were the ones that were like watching myself! Children do seem to be like walking reincarnations of their parents/grandparents, and so on, and whether that is us projecting onto them, or whether they really are like that person, is hard to disentangle. Certainly, if you are a parent you will have observed your parents' traits in your children and wondered how they got there!

I come down on the side of some genetic inheritance and some environment. Nature is combined with nurture for almost all of us. This debate is ongoing, as scientists regularly make claims through research.

The most important comment to make with regard to these difficult areas is that modelling always reaps more rewards than preaching. If we show a child through our life and actions what we expect of the child, they will indeed start to behave in what we regard as a "better" way. Better for us, and for the child. But to tell a child how to behave and then not carry that out in our lives is inconsistent and the child will always do as we do, not as we say. This is consciously explored through Godly Play – see chapter 8 – where good modelling is as important as anything else going on in the room.

Personality type indicators

Many adults reading this book will have used various tools that are now available to classify their own personality type. Probably the most popular of these at present is the **Myers-Briggs** personality type.[3] This system, which classifies people into one of sixteen types, was devised following basic Jungian typology and Jung's understanding of how they flourish. Myers and Briggs took the four Jungian aspects of personality and combined them. Two of the aspects are processes, one aspect is to do with attitude, and the other orientation.

The process options relate to situations and how we handle them. They are sensing versus intuition and thinking versus feeling. The attitude measure is judgment versus perception, and the orientation is extroversion versus introversion. The combinations are listed by the capital letters – for example, ENFJ, ISTP – and there are hence sixteen of these types. The letters indicate the person's preferred way of acting, but do not mean that they never use their shadow side. For example, while I am usually an extrovert, from time to time I enjoy time on my own, thinking things through. As I age, I am aware that the introversion is increasing, but I still operate as an extrovert in company. And after a day in front of my square screen I am keen to meet someone for a chat and social interaction. Each type will show a different personality and way of carrying out their lives and work. What it is critical for us to note is that this system can help us to see why that person drives me round the bend, and I can then work to understand why that person is acting in the way that they are, and that I am probably equally annoying and difficult for them. Once again, we see that everyone really is unique, and not likely to think or act as I do – and neither of those ways will necessarily be The Right Way. There is a real need to live and let live. If we can understand the different way that someone is working, then we can consciously come alongside them, working in our "shadow", and find ways to collaborate effectively.

There is a chart summarizing the differences below. If you find this interesting, you can find a basic test on the internet, which will give you a label, but you may find a day with an accredited Myers-Briggs specialist rather more helpful. Churches often have a Myers-Briggs workshop for their new church council. Bear in mind that your indicator is not fixed – I recently swung from an F to a T, much to my amazement. You can work on your shadow side to try and bring it into play more often, and if you are working with a similar type person, it's sometimes fun to stop and think how someone who has a very different way of interacting with your world would react to what you are planning! It's also important to recognize that with different personality types come preferred ways of worship, different prayer styles, different types of preferred music... There really isn't a "right" way to pray, I'm afraid, just the right way for you. Variety really is the spice of life here! And remember – you aren't "stuck" with this type for life; if there's something you don't like about your personality, get on with changing it by consciously choosing to use your shadow more often. There is no "better" type either – just how people are. You will prefer certain types, as they affirm you as a person and how you set about doing things, but life would be boring if we didn't have heated discussions, wouldn't it?

Preferred perception process (how I gather and process information) S or N

Sensing	iNtuition
Facts, multi-sensory	Abstract, symbol
Real, proven, known	Inspiration, hunch, possibilities
"Eyes tell mind"	"Mind tells eyes"

Preferred judging process (how I make decisions) T or F

Thinking	Feeling
Logical analysis	Personal consequences
Issues rather than feelings	Principles may be overlooked
Justice, what's fair	Emphasis on sympathy
Other's feelings may get hurt	

Preferred orientation (how I interact with the world) E or I

Extrovert	Introvert
Outer world, public, social	Inner world, privacy
Groups are energizing	Solitude is refreshing
Speak before I think	Think before I speak

Preferred attitude (how I undertake tasks) J or P

Judgment	Perception
Ordered, planned	Open, flexible
Likes closure, lists welcomed	Further information, other possibilities
Favours coming to clear decisions	Final decisions postponed

As with temperament, children can be seen to be developing these traits as they grow older. The trick is to aim towards a balance; while adults will always fall into these groups, if their score is near the boundary they are more balanced individuals.

Another aspect that will affect a child is that of the psycho-emotional growth that we each undergo. This was studied by Erik Erikson, and he developed a scheme that helps us to understand another aspect of what is going on in a person's life. Erikson worked as an analyst, and his system is again very helpful as we work with children, to give us a tool to try and understand the stresses and strains that our children are working on at any one point in time.

For about the first year of life, the child is engaged in **basic trust versus basic mistrust**: the child is learning to trust their mother/primary carer and learning about their own ability to make things happen. Mum/primary carer arrives if I cry, talks to me, and smiles in response to my smile. She continues to exist even when I can't see her, and always reacts to me in (roughly) the same way – with care and concern.

From about two to three, we see **autonomy versus shame**: the child is now mobile, and physical freedoms lead to them exercising free choice. They will go through toilet training, and the increasing sense of self-esteem will give them a lasting sense of pride and goodwill. If, however, this self-esteem is not there, because the child is being shamed and has self-doubts, the seeds of low self-esteem are sown in the person, and these may be hard to overcome. Their internal sense of justice also develops through their sense of autonomy.

At about the age of four to five, the child enters the stage called **initiative versus guilt**: the child at this age likes to organize their activities around clearly defined goals. They love to work with other children and learn rapidly – the "sponge-like" quality that is so attractive. There may be conflict with the same-sex parent, and this can lead to feelings of guilt in the growing child.

From about six to twelve years, the child is engaged in **industry versus inferiority**: working to absorb the norms of the culture that they are living in – all children engage in some learning at this point, no matter where they live. They are very concerned to make things – think of all those box sculptures that infant children bring home, the pictures on the fridge, and the storybooks of the older child. Their increasing aggressive drives go into a more dormant state, and the child may become very conformist.

From about thirteen to eighteen years, the adolescent period, the young person is in the stage called **identity versus role confusion.** There are many tasks for the adolescent to deal with: adapting to the physical changes that take place, making an occupational choice, or at least choosing if and where they go to study further, working towards an adult sexual identity, and searching for new values, which they feel are "theirs" and not those of the people whom they've been living with since birth. They may have to go once more through the fights of early childhood, with parents playing their adversary, albeit not wishing so to do. They take on idols, icons, and ideas as they move towards this more lasting identity, trying to integrate their personalities, taking from their childhood as well as the people with whom they now socialize. They may over-identify with certain groups, joining cliques or gangs as they express themselves over and against the child who they were. These young people will fall in love, while the sexual mores of the culture will determine how active they are sexually. They are also developing their own set of ethics and morality and tend to believe that really successful adults are also the "best" adults.[4]

Learning styles

This section of the chapter is entirely based on adult styles of learning. However, children are always learning and laying down their basic approach to life, so in the same way that their temperament will give a clue to adult personality, adult approaches to learning will give a clue retrospectively as to how children are learning. Watch a group of children and you can see the different styles developing very young! For example, some children won't do jigsaws, others prefer to play quietly on their own, entirely caught up in a different world, while others play as a gang. Different learning styles show people like to learn in different ways, and adults can be separated into four preferred styles of learning.

Activists

Activists are people who like a challenge, think variety is the spice of life, hope that learning is going to be enjoyable, and don't mind making mistakes. Activists bore quickly and "turn off". Activists can be quite difficult/challenging people to have in a group, as they will want it to move along at a good pace. They tend to have an extrovert personality. Child activists are often the first to put up their hand, and adult activists are the first to answer within a group.

An activist will approach learning with these questions:

- Will I learn something new?

- I do not want to sit for hours at a time doing nothing. Will there be a mixture of things to do?

- Will I be tied down to one particular subject or method, or are there options?

- Will there be some tough challenges for me to meet so I do not feel as if I am wasting my time?

- Will there be people like me on the course?

Reflectors

Reflectors don't like pressure or being in the spotlight. They may not be good at giving instant responses to groups or exercises, as they like to hear other people's views. This is important to bear in mind – don't ask them questions immediately within group work, give them time to process and then ask. They may have an introvert personality. A reflector will approach learning with these questions:

- Will I be given time to prepare and think things through properly or will I be put on the spot?

- Will there be a chance to do things properly, getting relevant information and thinking things through as we go along, or will it be all slap dash?

- Will we be steamrollered along a particular line, not encouraged to think for ourselves, but be given answers and information we have no opportunity to question?

- Will I get a chance to hear views of others in the group?

- If I am working alone, will I get enough time to do things properly? Do I have the support and encouragement of anyone outside the course?

Theorists

Theorists like being intellectually stretched and thrive on argument and discussion. They want to explore the structure of things, the theoretical base, and the thinking behind taken-for-granted assumptions. They may be either extrovert or introvert. A theorist will approach learning with these questions:

- Will I have a chance to question what's going on?

- Does the leaflet in front of me or the tutor of the course have a clear idea of what we are going to learn, how we are going to learn it and why, for instance, learning outcomes?

- Is this course going to be too easy for me? Will I only encounter ideas and arguments with which I am already familiar or will it take me further?

- Will there be people with my interests and approach there?

Pragmatists

Pragmatists likely to learn from successful people who have proved their competency in the field, rather than from ivory-towered experts. Again, they may be either extrovert or introvert. A pragmatist will approach learning with these questions:

- Will there be lots of practical tips and techniques?

- Will there be opportunities to practise?

- Have the people running the course shown that they know how to do this themselves?

- Is this course or event tackling real problems and some of my current concerns?

These learning styles are found in adults, but recently there has been a great deal of interest shown in children's learning styles: the Department for Education now recommends that children are taught in a variety of styles, but do not use the four classifications above. Instead, teachers now refer to VAK: visual, auditory, and kinaesthetic learning styles. Children who prefer **visual** learning would be good at old fashioned "chalk and talk", where the information is displayed and the teacher takes the child through. Worksheets, reference books, and online research are all examples of visual learning. **Auditory** learners focus on the sound of the lesson, be it from the teacher or something recorded, with the visual input less important. A **kinaesthetic** learner learns best when something active is involved, for example, role play. These children often find it hard to write up work, or to concentrate for long periods with a book.

VAK relates in some ways to the four adult styles, the most obvious being kinaesthetic relating to activist. There is still some debate over the value of the VAK system, but for me the important fact is that children learn best, as do adults, when the material is presented in a varied manner, so that each learning style is catered for, and the learners all have to use the styles that they may not prefer. That way we try to help learners to have a balance, and to also use the shadow styles.

Questions for discussion

1. What personality type are you? If you don't know, why not try out a Myers-Briggs workshop together? They're great fun as well as very helpful.

2. Do you have a favourite type of child – quiet, boisterous, outgoing, shy? Can you say what it is about that type of child that you enjoy?

3. This is something to do alone. What aspect of your personality do you dislike the most? What can you work on to help it to change? How will you pray about this?

4. How do you decide on the worship that your children experience? Should you widen the methods that you are using?

CHAPTER 4

Spiritual styles

*We were having a day using prayer stations, and we had
one set up with seashells. The children were told simply to
put the shell up to their ear and listen. "Mrs Darling," said
one, "I can hear God whispering to me!"*

Jackie Darling, retired primary school head

In September 2007, Dr Joyce Bellous[1] began supervising David
Csinos,[2] a post-graduate student working in local churches in
Canada as he examined the effect of the learning environment
upon children[3] during their sessions at church. He worked through
a small number of focus groups, which were made up of the
children at three local churches. He was not focusing on different
traditions, purely on what facilitated the children's participation
and spiritual growth during these sessions.

Through analysis of what the children said and fed back to him,
he came to recognize that there were effectively four ways "that
young people encounter God, participate in their congregations
and make meaning of the world around them."[4] Csinos and Bellous
called these four approaches "spiritual styles", and, working with
Denise Peltomaki, an expert in questionnaire design, a spiritual
styles questionnaire was designed so that others could participate
in this knowledge for themselves, and understand how the balance
of the four styles is seen throughout their whole lives. Csinos went
on to write the book *Children's Ministry That Fits*, a summary of his
dissertation.

Defining what the term "spiritual styles" means is quite difficult.
Bellous, in the introduction to the questionnaire, writes:

> *Your spiritual style conveys the way you try to improve a
> situation or make the world a better place... [It is] what
> people focus on as they make meaning out of life or carry*

out daily tasks... [It is] what really matters to people as they express what they believe... Assessing your Spiritual Style helps you to understand why people may be in conflict with one another even though those on each side of the disagreement are trying to be helpful... Assessing your Spiritual Style, and reflecting on the other styles, is one way to understand yourself better and to interpret the behaviour of others more effectively as you engage in common projects.[5]

If we are to minister well with children and young people, I believe a knowledge of spiritual styles is critical to our understanding of how both we and they tick, and how we prefer to worship. It will also make our sessions more inclusive and give us insight into how differently we all work and function as human beings. When I refer to "people" in this chapter, I am including all ages, from birth upwards.

It's perhaps most helpful to outline the characteristics of each style briefly. Most people are a blend of all four, some of three, but the prevailing style will be the one that drives an individual's behaviour and approach to life as a fully human being.

Word style

Traits found within people who favour the Word style are as follows:

- Word and accuracy are more important than aesthetics. Word style people are less concerned with the immediate environment or what something looks like. They focus in on the spoken or written word and will correct it to make the most fluent version.

- When the words are right, the world makes sense. They may ask people to explain themselves or be careful in the words they themselves choose to employ.

- Ethical living is of great significance. Emotion may not be understood as relevant to truth. Word people are good at ethics and can see through to the nub of a problem by analysis.

- Extreme cases don't recognize that thinking and feeling work together. Sometimes Word people can seem abrasive to other styles as they can be direct in their language.

- Their contribution to society is understood to come from intellectual wealth. Word people work hard to be as well educated as they can be, and value formal education highly.

- Could be described as "left brain" thinkers.

Word people within the church bring an ability to rationalize debate and cut through emotive language. They contribute to the ongoing development of theology, often at a high level, and are very helpful at committee work. Word children will often be found with a book or working hard to hone the language of a prayer they are writing. Word adults are often found in such fields as law or accountancy, and on high-level committees within a church structure, such as the General Synod in the Church of England.

Emotion style

Traits found within people who favour the Emotion style are as follows:

- Compassionate, relational people. Emotion style people are "people people" and relate well to others. They may have a well-developed intuition.

- They use language to express feelings rather than facts, which can present problems for Word style people. Their vocabulary may be used in a very different manner, expecting others to intuit their full meaning as well as the spoken meaning.

- Often charismatic leaders, Emotion people may refuse to be accountable for the hold they have over their peers. Emotion people don't always recognize how powerful they are as people, assuming that everyone could be that powerful too – if they actually consider this. In our context, Emotion style children may have a close set of friends over whom they unconsciously wield enormous influence.

- Decisions may be made following hunches, thus steering a group towards possible harm. Emotion people aren't usually as thorough or systematic in their decision making as Word people, so they may "jump" rather than consider.

- They will often clash with Word. This is not deliberate, but a reflection that the two styles think in very different ways and so can find that their language is causing the problem, not the motivation behind the words. They can feel insecure if in a group which is predominantly Word.

- Could be described as "right brain" thinkers.

Emotion people bring to the church an ability to worship through visual and performance arts, as well as powerful oratory. Thus Emotion children and young people are often keen to be involved in presenting dramas as sermons, or dance or use flags in worship. Emotion people love singing as part of a larger group, so these children and young people may join choirs. Classically, they find sermons almost impossible to journey with, getting distracted in the process, and may find the "best bit" of a service the coffee and fellowship at the end.

Symbol style

Traits found within people who favour the Symbol style are as follows:

- This person withdraws from trying to express outwardly what is perceived inwardly. Symbol people may not want to join in with debate, but to listen and observe.

- Life is a mystery, more felt than spoken. This means Symbol people find liturgy too wordy, and may prefer to be silent, taking in stillness and pausing while others may want to move on.

- Their spirituality combines emotion, symbol, solitude, ritual, and "the music of the spheres". They may have a strong attraction to less well-defined church traditions, or to those that have a high aesthetic such as Orthodox or Roman Catholic.

- They aim to form a connection with the world that doesn't need to be expressed through words.

- Symbol people may live in quiet and isolation.

- Symbol people love to be outside, in nature. They will often experience "awe and wonder", stopping to gaze at the sky or their environment.

Symbol people bring a sense of innate spirituality to the church. While they find group work more challenging than Word or Emotion people, they offer a different perspective on worship. How well they communicate with the other styles will depend on whether their Word or Emotion element is more present. Symbol people are not naturals in the church context, preferring to be out in nature to connect with God, walking in silence, or even gardening. Recent moves such as "walking church" or "forest/wild church" cater well for Symbol style people.

Action style

Traits found within people who favour the Action style are as follows:

- The overriding attitude is "what one *does*, not what one *says*". Thus value is given to others through what they actually give to the world, and Action people can be very perceptive in seeing through posturing by others.

- They have a strong desire for justice, acting for world-changing conditions. Action people work to change life for the better whenever they can, and this may significantly affect their choices.

- Single minded, passionate, observant, and impatient for change, Action people can be direct, and may become frustrated when other people can't understand or come alongside them in their impatience for change.

- Sometimes unable to express their needs through language, Action people may experience great frustration when thwarted.

Without Action people within our worshipping communities, nothing would get done! Action people drive the church forward and can be seen in many areas of Christian life volunteering and slowly bringing about change. Our Action children and young people are the ones who organize charitable events and get involved in them. They may well work for NGOs when they grow up or get involved in politics. They run our food banks, are street pastors, and may volunteer for organizations like Citizens Advice. Action children and young people mean that we can never just "tell a story", we always need to wonder together what the story means for us today – how does it challenge us, how does it impact our lives?

* * *

What is most important to state here is that there is little or no correlation between the styles and any other personality indicator that I have come across. For example, Active learners are not necessarily Action style. Extroversion/Introversion is visible across all four styles, although many Symbol people are more introverted *in my experience*. Other factors on the Myers-Briggs Type Indicator do not feature strongly in one style – it would seem to be something entirely different.

The implications of spiritual styles

It is in group work that the spiritual styles can be most evident, in the tensions when miscommunication arises, albeit without intent.

Think about those sessions with your children or young people at church or in school when one or two just don't "get" what's going on. Could that be due to their style? Or how about when you have an explosive argument within the group – is that two styles clashing? If it is, it's often Word and Emotion. Do you have someone who seems to exist in a different world to the others? They may be Symbol and needing reassurance that they're fine. If the person in charge of your worshipping community is Word – and they often are – they will be better at strategy and management than people skills. The trick is to make sure you also have an Emotion person working with them to form a good balance. If you work with children and young people, chances are that your predominant style is either Emotion or Action, which makes absolute sense if you think about it.

We all "hear" people from within our own style and find those of other styles more difficult - and that is why having an awareness of spiritual styles will help us all navigate sessions more successfully, with more positive outcomes.

How spiritual styles can help

A minister who knows their spiritual style will be an educated and reflective minister who has some idea of how the group functions, and the children/young people that self-select to come to the sessions, because it's highly likely that they share their spiritual style, and thus communications flow effortlessly. You will have sat down and worked out where the four styles will rub up against each other in an unhelpful way and have strategies ready that will help facilitate a concise and helpful meeting.

Word people, of all the styles, will predominate at any session, simply because they find them easier to negotiate. They like a concise, well-constructed session that has a structure which tells them exactly where the session will go; learning outcomes in school make absolute sense to them. (A well-planned session is helpful for everyone, but Word people will gain more security than those with another predominant style.)

Word people like a well-facilitated session and will struggle with those who get distracted or run off on a tangent. They find it hardest to put themselves into the mindset of the other styles, so they may get impatient with other styles if they're struggling.

Emotion leaders won't have prepared as well as the Word people, even if they have a high "J" on the Myers-Briggs indicator. Emotion people find learning outcomes far harder work to engage with and will be working in their "shadow". If the facilitator is an Emotion person, then they need to apply themselves and work in their shadow style, no matter how hard it is. If Emotion people lead sessions and allow their Emotion side to dominate, you will have frustrated Word people who feel the session could be far better led. Expect lots of the group to be Emotion people, and these can be taken along by passionate oration, so if a Word person indicates you are all getting a bit carried away then you must listen to them. Remember, Word and Emotion people may find it difficult to hear one other. Always make sure that you repeat badly worded questions, editing the language to enable the Word people to hear it more clearly, but checking that you haven't changed the Emotion person's meaning. Older Emotion people may realize that they use language in a looser way, and won't mind being "tidied up" a little, in my experience. But if the facilitator is an Emotion person, they will have to be monitoring themselves very carefully, and might want a co-leader who can do the "Emotion-Word" translation, and who has been well briefed in this aspect of the task.

Symbol people may not be there at all. Symbol people find most religious events difficult due to the lack of silence and predominance of the spoken word. Try to check with them as much as you tactfully can. The Symbol person brings a different perspective but may be struggling with the session more than anyone else there. Keep an eye on them, and if they want to make a contribution, make sure you give them the opportunity, as they will be speaking for a small, quiet but observant minority. Starting the session with a period of silent prayer will help a Symbol person to centre themselves in the group, and pausing from time to time, to consider what's just been said/suggested, will give Symbol people a pause to process. Pausing will also take the emotion out of the moment for everyone else, so all benefit from what the Symbol person brings. Giving time for everyone to respond via a creative medium is always a good idea, and Symbol people can work on where they are in the session physically to great benefit – as can everyone else!

It is important to be aware that Symbol young people may well be aware that they don't function according to the church group norm and feel that they are "wrong" in some way. It is very important that you encourage them to recognize that they are a loved child of God, and that they bring an unusual and much-valued perspective to the group. It is OK to be an introvert who likes to think and reflect in silence!

Action people can get very frustrated by the process. They will be looking for the action points in the session and could become increasingly bored and detached. You can help an Action person to relate by stressing what your group has achieved. Make sure that you evaluate, reflecting on what has happened and what the visible results have been, as well as those results that are less easy to measure in a quantifiable way. Ensure that you value the input of the Action people, as they may well be the driving force behind your group. These are the people who often lead the work with children and young people, so reflect on how Action leaders are fed spiritually, as often they spend their lives giving.

If you can use these basic tools to help your groups work well with one other and with you, you will greatly enable the sometimes difficult process of being church together.

Shadow styles

If a person completes the questionnaire to ascertain their spiritual style, they get a value for each of the styles, with the highest number indicating their spiritual style. So, for example, you may score 16 Word, 10 Emotion, 4 Symbol, and 6 Action. This makes you a Word person. Or you could be 16 Emotion, 10 Word, 5 Symbol, and

5 Action, which would mean you were an Emotion person, and so on. Very occasionally, someone comes out at 9 each, a perfect balance (as the questions add up to a total of 36), so those people need to look at the personality traits listed previously and decide which is their dominant style by using the descriptors to find themselves (or asking their nearest and dearest, who may be more aware than the person themselves.) Sometimes one of the styles is completely absent, and that's fine.

You should then find your shadow style. Word and emotion are the shadow of each other. If you are either Symbol or Action style look at the style that came "last", the one with the lowest value, and that gives you the style that you are least at home with – and that will be your shadow.

Take a look at the characteristics of your shadow style and analyze how to work and act as if you had that style. That may seem very challenging indeed but bearing your shadow style in mind while leading a group can be a very helpful, but demanding, and costly experience. It also moves each person towards a more balanced, overall style, with greater empathy for all. Jesus moved between all four, harnessing energy to meet each situation in the best way. This is what we are aiming for in working with our shadow.

For the individual, knowing your own style, and anticipating where dysfunction may occur in communication, through no one's fault, is very helpful. Emotion people can concentrate on speaking clearly to Word people, and Word people can recognize the problems they may have in clearly comprehending what an Emotion person is saying. Symbol people have to work hard on their shadow style, to persevere and recognize the value they contribute, no matter how difficult such a meeting is for them. They will also have to work hard to keep themselves present in the meeting rather than losing themselves in thought. Action people need to sit on their hands and recognize that many people have to go through a seemingly tedious and wordy process before anything ever gets done!

Knowing our own style will help every individual feel more at ease with themselves, and help us to recognize where difficulty is coming from and how to smooth it over honestly. A session without disagreements is a pipe dream and would be ineffective. Honest debate and openness to each other engenders growth in an adult fashion. Spiritual styles offer an enormous amount to everyone present in such meetings and to the spiritual growth process itself.

In summary, if you are Word, then you find Emotion and Symbol people most difficult. If you are Emotion, you find Word people most difficult. Symbol and Action will depend on your own questionnaire "score" within those styles. Symbol people often find Word most difficult, followed by Action and Emotion or vice versa. Action people will vary according to their Emotion/Word measure but will always look for a positive outcome.

Environmental influences on spiritual styles

There is no doubt in my mind that we are born predisposed towards one of the styles as dominant, however, human beings are social animals, and how we treat each other always has some degree of gender expectation underlying it, no matter how carefully we act. If you are not persuaded by this, go to a toy shop of any kind and look at the marketing and the gender-specific toys on sale. In blind tests, where adults are asked to interact with babies, girls will be treated differently to boys, and there is still an expectation of how women and men behave as adults as well as children and young people. So how does this impact upon our style?

Having worked with spiritual styles for about ten years, it seems to me that men who are under forty are more likely to identify as Emotion than older men. If you think about the revolution that has taken place over childcare and mental health over the last decades, the reign of the "stiff upper lip" men has gone. We now hear members of the royal family talking about mental health issues and vulnerability, even changing royal babies' nappies (although I expect the nanny might be doing that more frequently!). It is OK now for men to be in touch with their "feminine side" in a way that would have been anathema to my father and his generation. I find more men of the baby boom generation and older to be Word than men who are Generation X. Is this because the younger men have been "allowed" to be themselves in this way, and not channelled towards the more Word approach to life? Likewise, it is now far easier for women who are naturally Word to be themselves, not squeezed towards the more caring skills of the Emotion style that has been regarded as "women's work". Similarly, I wonder if Symbol children force themselves into a more "usual" style, as teachers try to engage them with more friends and parents worry about their solitary nature. When I lead spiritual styles workshops, it is the Symbol people who tend to sigh with relief as they discover they are fine, just unusual. And maybe Symbol isn't unusual at all, just hidden? It's certainly not common in church-going people, although the numbers of Symbol clergy are increasing – a very positive step, albeit unconscious from those who select.

We shall see as the next generation starts to show who they really are.

Questions for discussion

You may be thinking, "But I'm a mixture of all of the styles." That's correct – you are, but it may be worth you completing a questionnaire to find your balance. (In the UK, to the best of my knowledge, I am the only person with questionnaires.)

1. How will you change your planning to accommodate all four styles?

2. Will this knowledge affect the way you plan "all age" worship?

3. How do we see these styles in the gospel accounts of Jesus' life?

4. Do you think we can see predominant styles in each of the four gospel writers?

CHAPTER 5

Social development

*I think about God when I'm scared, like the time my dad
told me to go downstairs and my brother scared me.*
Isabella, six years old

This chapter is about the social skills that we all learn, some during
our childhood and some as we grow older, as some social skills are
picked up in later life. For us, the important thing to recognize is
that we do indeed learn these skills, even though we will have no
memory of doing so for most of them. For us as adults, working
with children and young people, we need to be aware that we
may have expectations that are totally at odds with some of our
children's life experiences, and this will affect how we interact
with our young charges. Our expectations are deep-seated and
"invisible" a great deal of the time; it is only when we realize we
are finding a particular child (or adult) difficult that we stand
back, analyze what's going on here, and recognize the disjunction
between us. So let's consciously think about some of these invisible
factors that may be at work.

Socialization

Socialization is one of those things that you're only aware of when
it goes wrong; a bit like your central heating system. And like that
central heating, socialization often breaks down at Christmas!
Socialization refers to the system by which we pick up the "normal"
way of behaving. It's usually unnoticed and always assumed to be
common to all in a group, and it's only when someone goes beyond
or outside of the rules of the group that we become aware of the
subtle processes that keeps society and groups together. We learn
rules of behaviour such as not speaking over other people, not
leaving a restaurant without paying the bill, not throwing rubbish

on the floor, or wiping feet or removing shoes on entering a house…
and you can't remember how you did that learning. You "just know".
We usually conform to group norms without noticing that they are
there. Some people clearly find it easier to speak out against a group
than others; those who chair committees will be aware of that, and
we all know such people and may quietly envy them their "thick
skin" when it comes to saying what they think despite the feeling
that the rest of the group have or have gone along with. Likewise,
we have all been in a group where there is a newcomer, who doesn't
know how the group works, and may speak and act in a way that we
find disturbing but cannot quite articulate why. Unless that person
works out the difference, they may find themselves being quietly,
and probably unintentionally, squeezed out.[1]

Does this conformity come from that most ancient of causes,
survival instinct? I think it does. If a pack or herd animal is alone,
outside of the group, it is likely to be picked off by a predator and
eaten. And those who are outside of the dominant social group
of humans are just as likely to be picked upon and "devoured"
by the big people who set the rules of what is "normal". We see it
in nurseries, where some children are excluded from the group,
often for reasons adults cannot fathom at all. As children move up
through school, they may have the wrong type of school jumper,
and we know about designer trainers and so forth. The pros and
cons of social media and the effect it has on children and young
people is debated endlessly. I can remember a girl when I was
about nine whom we ostracized because she was "square"; she
had absolutely no fashion sense at all, neither did she conform to
many of the other social mores that our group held.[2] Adults are
not above this sort of behaviour: colour, sexuality, gender, slavery;
all of these were legally discriminated against until strong people
stood up against the crowd. Many are still discriminated against in
the wider population, with subtle behaviours that continue unless
challenged either internally by the conscience, or externally by
someone speaking out. Your church will have different groups
too, where people with the same interests and lifestyles tend to

congregate. You know, the "choir" group, the "servers" group, possibly the "Sunday school teachers" group, and so on.

Groupthink

People who challenge the social norms are standing against a factor called "groupthink". I know it sounds like something from Orwell's *1984* but it's a powerful force, and one to be recognized and reckoned with. Groupthink is the social pressure to conform to what a group is thinking. So, if you go to a BNP rally, it's hard to speak of an inclusive multicultural country in a positive light. If you're at a black-tie dinner, chances are you're wearing a rather swanky suit or a posh frock. My husband took great delight in not wearing a tie to a Buckingham Palace garden party (one of the perks of my previous post), but other than a (female) Canadian "Mountie" I didn't see any women in trousers, although a few (clergy) men were wearing frocks! Although I'm joking here about groupthink, it's a very strong force. Perhaps the worst example I know is about the committee that met to decide whether to launch a certain space shuttle on a very frosty morning. The ice caused the "O-rings" to fail, and the shuttle, Challenger, exploded on launch. One man alone said this would happen and desperately tried to persuade the others on the launch committee to postpone. As you know, everyone on board that shuttle died, and the programme was grounded for years as a result.

Groupthink often means that a group of individuals agree together to do something that none of them would even consider as an individual. Ever find yourself wondering just how you agreed to do that task at the last church meeting? Was this how you became Sunday school superintendent, or whatever you call that role in your church?

Freud held that socialization was achieved through the repression of children, forcing them to conform to the roles and norms of adults. This is not generally held to be so, but some socialization certainly can be repressive. The film *School of Rock* gives a great example of a very smart, American private school accidentally employing a rock guitar player as a music teacher, and how his encouraging the children to play rock music rather than classical helped them to break out of the repressive expectations of their parents.[3] Don't get me wrong, I love classical music, but a good blast of Led Zeppelin works differently on the psyche.[4] And those kids needed to let their hair down and enjoy being what they were – kids.

Children are not born with a working model of the society into which they have been born. It is clearly up to others to teach them. How deep that teaching goes is questionable, as in books such as *The Lord of the Flies*, or what we see happening in states of war.[5] However, in "normal" times, societies exist and are clearly different across the globe. A multinational bank runs TV advertisements about what is acceptable in one culture being unacceptable in others – it's one of the joys of foreign travel. If you have ever been to the Far East, to a country such as Japan, you will know that the different culture is absolutely incomprehensible at first, but after a few days you find yourself bowing to people as well as lining up on the station platform in exactly the right spot for that carriage of the Shinkansen (bullet train). Jon Sopel's recent book *If Only They Didn't Speak English* is a brilliant exposition on the differences between Trump's America and the UK.[6]

It seems to me that only people who speak English as a second language reply "You're welcome" when I thank them! Each culture has its own ways of being and doing. The novel *One Big Damn Puzzler* gives a brilliant insight into a foreigner living and working abroad.[7] One of the norms was you shouldn't share a house with anyone of the opposite sex if you weren't married. Sex outside of marriage was rife, but they never stayed for breakfast with their lovers.

Research into socialization

It was the advent of video recording that gave those researching social development the biggest leap forward, as children could now be watched without setting up laboratory conditions, which nearly always give skewed results. As a result of this, the "mutuality model" was proposed.[8] This says that the child is an active participant in their social development, stressing their *inter*dependence with their adult carer for many of their social interactions. While adults like to think they're teaching the child, the child actually has more control in this process than we recognize. But note – no researcher has ever said that there won't be stresses and conflicts during this process. Tantrums are official! Through a whole gamut of exploration and stimuli, the child learns and progresses socially. Children are not a blank slate at birth; they bring their own predispositions, capacities, and reflexes. Any parent will tell you that their children were born with the makings of the person they become, that all children, even identical twins, are very different. They may have a "laid back" personality in contrast to their big sister's much more "up and at 'em" approach to life. While a child responds to the people and the world around them, they do it from varying starting positions.

All children are particularly attuned to other human beings. Put a child in a room and they will go to the people rather than the library books – perhaps taking an adult to the books but often finding the person first. Children prefer people who talk and move to those who sit like a statue in silence (don't we all?). That's why babies seem to almost expect to be entertained by adults. That's what we do automatically.

We are all predisposed to prefer human voices to any other sounds, and adults will tune in to a small child before a larger one. Bring a newborn into a room and watch everyone focus on the baby. We can't help it. And, as we get older, we maintain the tendency to see faces in many things; look at the "I saw Jesus in my beer foam" stories in the press, the faces you see before you go to sleep. See how we hold young babies too – at face-to-face level, which actually gives a fairer power dynamic. We are looking straight into the baby's eyes, but she can turn her head away if she so desires and make us work to catch her attention. If you watch the way adults talk to babies, you may notice the way that by about six months, the child is being given a space to reply, even though she doesn't speak. Chatting in this way with very small children gives them the turn-taking practice that will enable conversation later on.

Development of relationships

John Donne commented that "No man is an island, entire of itself," and he was absolutely right.[9] We are always searching for other people. Human beings are relational beings, and that is the interpretation many modern theologians have of being made in the image of God. How those relationships develop has been studied carefully. The first relationships that we develop will be with those who care for us, and as we go through life the quality of those first relationships will affect the quality of ones that we form later. You really can blame your parents! A specific, enduring tie between two humans is called an **attachment**, and with young children evidence of an attachment is given through the child preferring that person's attention, touching, clinging to them, crying for them if they're not there, smiling at them when they are. You will instinctively recognize when that relationship is healthy, and likewise alarm bells will ring when you see a parent with a child when they do not share a healthy relationship. Our first attachment can be observed very early on, but from six months it is quite marked. It's necessary at the start of life, or who would feed, care for, and protect this young person? Animals clearly exhibit attachments in the same way as humans. Emperor penguins and seahorses are known for the extreme parenting skills of the male. Elephants have been known to remain in the area where their young perished, and attack the object that caused the death, as in a case where a baby elephant was killed by a train and the mother "haunted" that area of track, causing mayhem in her grief. But few animals care for their young in the extended way that humans do.

One of the key researchers in this field was John Bowlby, who worked just after the Second World War, looking at how evacuation had affected children, and then looking at how children who had been hospitalized away from their carers were affected.[10] All over the world, researchers have recognized three different styles of attachment. I use "mother" here to represent the key carer, although clearly it may be other people who are significant in the child's rearing.

- **Anxious/avoidant.** A child who has this style of attachment will show little distress when her mother leaves and shows equally little interest when her mother returns. Approximately 20 per cent of the population exhibits this style.

- **Securely attached.** In these cases, the child actively seeks to maintain proximity to her mother. When her mother is present, the child will actively explore and interact with other people and objects. She will be distressed if her mother departs and will greet her mother enthusiastically on return. Approximately 70 per cent of the population demonstrate this style of attachment.

- **Anxious/ambivalent.** This child shows distress when her mother leaves, but will resist contact when she returns, and may display anger during their reunion. About 10 per cent of the population exhibit this style. (But about 75 per cent of the characters in the soap operas we know and love so well have this less stable attachment style, otherwise there wouldn't be the same amazing storylines.)

There is much evidence that it is to the individual's advantage to have the second style of attachment. These people score higher on tests in interpersonal confidence and cognitive development, play more with toys as children, explore more willingly and in a healthier manner, and show a greater eagerness to learn. The provision of a secure base in this first relationship has implications for later relationships. We continue to form attachments right throughout our life, and they are important to us; the pattern of our early relationships will become the model for those we form later. Expectations of relationships vary with the original style of attachment: Anxious/ambivalent adults are more uncertain about their relationships, and may worry that their partner doesn't love them, leading to the breakdown of the partnership, not helped by their own inconsistent displays of emotion. Avoidant lovers will find any close relationship uncomfortable and they will be reluctant to commit.

When we look at people's orientation towards society, we discover that the quality of attachment towards a father will affect how patriotic a child may become. Those with a secure attachment will love their country, but an insecure attachment will give a child a tendency towards preoccupation with national dominance. Perhaps of most interest to this book, some research implied that the quality of this first attachment will give differing styles of religious commitment in that those with secure attachment will find it easier to have a good understanding of God, whereas those with less security may have an exclusive "me and God" style of faith, which is very critical of ministers and the church community.[11]

Other research has shown that those with a secure attachment cope with trauma by seeking help from others, while those who are ambivalent will become emotionally volatile, and the avoidants will try to distance themselves psychologically from events.

The development of language

Inevitably, there is a great deal of interest in the process by which we develop language. It's clearly a very sophisticated process, and children take quite a while to pick up grammar as well as vocabulary. A toddler will presume how to make a plural of a word, saying mouses or mans rather than mice and men. They will say that they runned rather than ran, and children can be quite difficult to get to use the correct, acceptable form of the language. There is no doubt that what they learn is related to a specific context and social experiences; a child will not offer vocabulary to do with an office block unless they have experienced either a book/story about this, been taken there, or somehow come across that environment. Likewise, a child in Britain is not likely to know about life in Ancient Rome unless they have been specifically told about it. They pick up intonation, vocabulary, phrasing, and accent from the people they hear speaking, and this can be very specific to a small area.

Children learn about *reciprocity* – taking it in turns to contribute to a conversation – early in their lives. This pattern gives rise to dialogue, but small children can find waiting their turn very difficult.

Parents work hard with their child to give vocabulary and language within a shared context. How many hours do most parents spend reading to their child, so increasing their vocabulary and knowledge of speech? It has been observed that parents will take a lead on their subject matter by monitoring the interest level of the child. Mine loved to talk about all sorts of things, but the finer details of theology had to wait a while. Carers will also give a format for language, for example, in reading a picture book, the adult will point and say, "That's a boat, that's a car, that's a train," each time the "that's a" working as a signal that the really important word, the noun, is the one to learn, as that's the one that changes as the picture changes. Carers will also unconsciously be monitoring the level of interest that the child shows as they chat and will skew the conversation towards the subjects that the child is interested in. So if a child is playing with their trains, that's what the carer will chat about. If the carer is talking to the child about the dog and a horse trots by, catching the child's attention, then the chat will shift to horses, and so on.

You will have noticed that we use a different tone of voice when speaking to young children. We raise the pitch, we speak more slowly, and we change the emphasis. This can be called "parentese" or child-addressed speech. I'm afraid I use the same style with my dog. But we simplify the language and so simplify the task of learning, just as I would do if I ever had to teach someone a new language. I don't want to learn French from someone speaking at their normal speed and using all sorts of complicated grammatical structure; "*Jean écoute la radio,*" slowly and precisely will do! Likewise, it's thought that children acquire the framework for language before vocabulary.

There are clearly some problems with the above theory. I speak parentese to my dog, and while he's got me well trained to understand certain looks (he's waiting for tea as I type, and we both know that I know what he wants!), he's never opened his mouth and asked me, "Please could I have tea now?" And while some birds can copy words – no examples here for obvious reasons – they never come out with words in a sentence unless they've been drilled previously.

Children all seem to learn language at about the same time no matter where they live. A Russian toddler will be making the same sorts of babbling noises as the toddler in my local deli is at present, but while the Russian child will speak Russian, my deli toddler will speak English, with a smattering of Greek and Italian. But there has yet to be a toddler who could speak who grew up in isolation. We need others around us to model how to do it. Tarzan had to learn how to say "Me Tarzan, you Jane" as an adolescent. What is now recognized is that children who grow up hearing more than one language, such as in a mixed-race relationship, fluently speak both languages and can differentiate, and this also has a huge impact on other areas of learning as the bilingual effect seems to affect other areas of the brain.

There is a huge debate about how we learn to speak, and it's now believed by many that we are born to speak, as we are born to walk upright. What we learn is the language and dialect of speech, but that speech is somehow instinctive.

Acquiring language is a truly stunning feat, one that we have all mastered without thinking about it. While I may wish I had a wider vocabulary, I manage to communicate OK. And here's an obvious comment that you may not have thought of before; language is a tool. If you don't use it, it is useless! A conversation is an amazing social interaction of expression and impression.

Think of the conversations you've had today. Sometimes we do have to reiterate as we've rushed to the point without keeping our audience with us, but overall isn't it stunning? Language is a task that we have never come to the end of; think of all those words you don't know! We continue learning throughout our lives, not only technical jargon that's being invented, but the rich vocabulary in which we are immersed. Language is the medium through which we teach (although only 10 per cent is spoken, the rest is taken in subconsciously through body language). We tell stories, we ask and answer questions, we assert our authority, we say what's what and whose coat that is... and while the style of our language informs other listeners a great deal about us, without language we would not be doing what we do for so much of the time.

You will have noticed, too, how quickly accents change when families move area. My children were born in Nottingham and had hard vowel sounds until we moved to Hertfordshire. Within a few months, my daughter was posh estuary. My son took longer to stop saying "one" in the northern manner. When we moved round London to Kent, the accent switched oh so subtly to Kent estuary English. Now my son is in York, I wonder what he'll sound like soon. Listen to me speak and you'll probably ask me where I come from, for I have a north midland vowel sound that just comes through from time to time, though I can't hear it. My first teaching job was in a mining area of Nottinghamshire. I lived in the city, and had no problem with that dialect at all, but when I started in this particular school, I thought I'd entered a foreign country. When I asked a child where his homework was, he replied, "It's a tom" (It's at home). It took me weeks to pick up this very local but very dense dialect. The children thought I was French, because the other teacher with RP vowels was actually German, and my name sounded foreign. And we are not alone. The Queen has also come downmarket in her accent over the fifty years of Christmas broadcasts. David Cameron and George Osborne both have glottal stops, which I'm sure they didn't learn at Eton. Gangs use language to set them apart, with their own "in-house" dialect. I won't go into texting or the use of emojis!

Our understanding of the world is affected by our understanding of our language. We cannot underestimate how critical it is.

Many years ago, I worked in a UPA (Urban Priority Area) with young people and adults' groups. One of the women's groups had a crèche, with qualified speech therapists. The local schools were finding the children in their nursery class and upwards violent, and they realised that it was because the children found communication with their teachers hard – because they couldn't articulate their needs through recognized speech – so speech therapists were trying to provide a richer language environment for these children to help. This was a case of proactive therapy, to save more expensive intervention later on. And it worked.

This raises a very important area for us as communicators; there are many forms of speech, and I tend to believe that I do it properly. So if a child comes to Sunday school and is silent, it may not be because they have a poor command of English; it may be that their English is different from mine. Put them into a safe environment, and they'll chatter away furiously, but the language I'm using is different from that of their home environment, and that does not make mine correct, and theirs wrong, just different. We will both need time together to come to a compromise, and we'll do it without noticing.

Body language

Most of us are now familiar with the basic concept of body language – that we speak far more loudly with our bodies than we do with our mouths, and that we are subconsciously responding to someone's body language all the time. Take the standard situation: Suzie has been naughty and you are about to tell her off. You'll take a deep breath, and your body will expand. You may cross your arms. Your voice will change tone and pitch, and Suzie will see this and mentally brace herself before you've opened your mouth. Or you're going to praise Suzie for her fantastic story: You'll smile, right up to your eyes, and possibly lean back or to one side. Again, Suzie knows what's coming before you open your mouth. Watch a couple of women in a coffee shop as they chat. (Sorry, but women do this better than men, as a generalization.) They will lean in towards each other, and their bodies will tend to mirror each other. Their heads could be quite close together... and off they go, taking turns and just sensing when it's their time to join in. I once sat in a clergy meeting with the local MP, who was a cabinet minister at the time. I could not work out why something was ringing alarm bells in my head until quite a while afterwards; what he said was OK, he seemed nice enough, but I realised that he had sat in a perfectly body neutral manner, legs straight out in front, feet flat on the floor, hands on knees, and he hadn't moved. There was no body language coming off the guy and he felt like a talking dummy. We need body language to give us the rest of the story. Deaf people who lip-read say that they need to be face on, but the real story is in the rest of the body as we talk to one other.

Like language and dialect, body language is localized. I know that a Greek person is likely to be far more bodily active than me when I chat with him. Italians – well, they like to be dramatic, as do Spaniards. Gross generalizations here, but you get my drift. But if you are talking with someone from another culture, it could be that your body language confuses them, as one gesture may have a very different overtone in their language or dialect – pointing fingers is a prime example. Universities now have departments to look after overseas students who are studying for UK degrees, and part of the teaching involved is the local body language, so that the students can "read" a situation more easily. So, do be aware that someone coming into your group from outside the area may be struggling to get up to speed with body language just as much as verbalization.

Understanding people and society

If we are to function within society, we need to be able to take in all sorts of information about the other people we are working and living with. Every child needs to grasp that people are unique; everyone is different and will react differently. We all look different too, and we have a store of recognition data to enable us to recognize the right person before we throw ourselves into their arms. Have you experienced that lovely moment of having a toddler attach itself to you, look up, and realize that you're the wrong pair of legs? How do I learn who has the same sense of humour as I do? This is vital knowledge if I'm not to get it really wrong socially; where to draw the line is a very variable point. Yet we cannot observe mental activity, just its merest glimmerings on another person's face, but a toddler soon learns how to read that face. Children learn to watch and read non-verbal language at a very early age, and to gauge what's going on beneath the surface. We still do not understand how we acquire this understanding, but it seems that younger children read physical appearance more than older children, who will speak about personality rather than physical descriptions.

During middle childhood the understanding of these fine mechanisms increase, and the concept of friends, friendships, and mutual responsibilities, and the obligations of peers develops. Children as young as five can predict how people that they know well will respond, which shows an understanding that other people are thinking, remembering, and perceiving. Learning this skill seems to depend on the child's social context and listening to other people speaking about their own social interactions. As the child grows older, so the awful reality of social embarrassment appears. It seems almost as if the parent and the child are one unit, as a parent's embarrassment will lead to the child sharing the emotion. Much of this social embarrassment can be seen in situations where other people think that "the child should know better"; those of us with tall children will know the feeling well. I remember taking a christening where the child, who was only eleven months but was very big and running around, behaved appallingly. When people realized he wasn't two or three years old, but actually not even one, they rapidly revised their opinions... well, some did.

Children also have to learn all about the social structures of their culture. It's within their family that they learn about religion and faith life lived in the community. It's their families that teach them about shops and how they work, with many children believing that there's no end to the money in that machine in the wall, and that shopkeepers magic up their goods behinds the scenes! Needless to say, as children grow older, so their understanding increases in its sophistication. This social awareness is very localized, giving rise to the amazing variety of cultures that we now see across the globe and indeed within many countries.

Generational theory

Through the last century, research began to point out the differences between the generations and establish how these came about. If you want to really understand this quite straightforward theory, I suggest you read the book *Mind the Gap*, which also gives insights into why we have such expressions as "Generation X", or "baby boomers".[12] While this is a theory, there are clear differences in the way that people from different generations tend to live and think, and we need to be aware of how we may not react in the same way as someone who is thirty years older or younger than us, due to the differences in our lives when we were children. "Gen theory" will help you to understand why some people are more conservative in their views, as well as looking at how different generations have had to cope with different demands, which impact their attitudes and life choices. Our current group of children are known as "Generation Z" and we are yet to see how growing up under austerity affects them as adults.

The whole area of social development is huge and somewhat stunning to think about. We've barely scratched the surface here but I hope that this chapter has given you food for thought and enabled you to challenge some of the givens for your group and society.

Questions for discussion

1. Which groups do you belong to? How important are they to you? Can you imagine life alone?

2. Have you been aware of groupthink operating in a group that you belong to? Was that a good or bad experience?

3. How would you like to shift the thinking within your church? How could you try to achieve that shift?

4. Are you aware of judging people by their speech? Are there any dialects that you find unpleasant? Can you work out why?

5. How can you help to socialize the children in church more effectively, without repressing them?

CHAPTER 6

Faith and how it grows

*I don't know what God looks like but I know that he is
powerfall (sic) and wise.*
Elspeth, eight years old

If you were to ask a group of people what they thought the word
"faith" means, you'd probably have as many meanings of the word
as people in the room. My thesaurus has the following:

*Confidence, trust, reliance, assurance, conviction, belief,
devotion, loyalty, faithfulness, commitment, dedication.*

Your group would probably have meanings with religious overtones,
as do many of those above. If you followed up that question with
what the role of the church was, and by implication your children's
work, then "faith" would probably reckon in the answers to that
second question. Helping people to find faith, to grow their faith, to
have their faith develop, are all part of the agenda at most churches.

Over the last fifty years, academics have been working at the
concept of "faith" and trying to make schemes of how faith grows
in human beings. There are recognized names in the field, and I
would like to look at the work of four of them: James Fowler, John
Westerhoff, Sarah Brush, and Sandy Eisenberg Sasso. Both Fowler
and Westerhoff have worked and written extensively in this field
and come up with systems that help us to understand and recognize
the changes and development in the faith that we share with those
who we live and work with. Both men recognized that their work
produced tools to give insight. Neither claimed that these schemes
are perfect, and both acknowledged that many people do not
easily "fit" the potential boxes that the schemes give us. Fowler and
Westerhoff worked at Harvard University in the 1970s onwards, but
the schemes are applicable to those people within the developed

world who live in what are, or were, broadly Christian societies. Fowler died in 2015, but Westerhoff is still alive and travelling, sharing his ideas.

Sarah Brush's ideas are very recent and are a metaphoric rather than a psychological construct. She was working with the insight of history and in response to the two earlier theories. Sandy Eisenberg Sasso is an American rabbi, who writes and teaches from her perspective about faith and our human experience of God.

The insight that each theory gives will ring true in many cases, but it must always be born in mind that these theories are not proven fact. They are tools to help us understand the processes of a person's spiritual development. It is important to note that Fowler uses the word "faith" as a psychological construct in his definitions and theory rather than a theological term, so you may find the following needs thinking about carefully, with their various meanings of "faith" high in your consciousness. It is also worth taking on board that Fowler's research work focused more on adults than children. This may take authority away from his discussion of faith development in children, but what he has to say is nevertheless important. His concentration on adults was mainly because adults are easier to interview as they are more articulate. He may also have been influenced by working in a time when children's spirituality was rarely reckoned as important. Brush uses the term in the context of Christian faith development, and her ideas were based on an online survey and with experience of working as a Diocesan youth adviser, which she then reflected upon to produce a metaphor for faith development that scientists in particular might find appealing.

As I have already said, faith is hard to define. I sometimes say it is a slippery concept, wide and inclusive. You might like to think of it like a shawl – something that we wrap round our shoulders to keep us warm and fight off the cold. But that speaks more of a property of faith than of what it actually is – back to the difficulty of an agreed definition.

To give faith this clear function, that of protector, warmth, a covering that we own, is a very emotive expression, and hints at how personal faith is understood to be by the modern Western person. Faith, in Fowler's terms, is an internal concept to which we attach great importance in our understanding of who we are as individuals. Modern people may find his use of "faith" overlaps with their concept of "spirituality". Fowler states that all people have faith, although it may not be religious – he speaks of faith as a recognition that there is more to life than just the physical and while that may involve belief in the transcendent, that may not be what you or I would name as "God". If our faith involves trust and a loyalty towards that transcendent being so that we develop religious faith, then we will indeed speak of "God" and having faith in that God.

You may be thinking, "So what's the difference between faith and spirituality?" and that is a good question. For me, faith is less emotive or intuitive and more conscious; something that you tease at mentally, working on as a kind of personal philosophy of life. Spirituality includes our deepest emotions – love, joy, grief, as well as how we relate to each other, which is, in my experience, rarely rational! Perhaps faith is a verb, an action, while spirituality is an experience of an inner life.

Fowler's assertion that all people have faith is widely held amongst people working in the fields of faith development or spirituality; you will remember the comments in chapter 1 regarding Alister Hardy's work in the area of spirituality/religious experience, and how that religious experience has survival value to the individual, which is now regarded as trailblazing for my generation and that which preceded us. He did not refer to faith, but to a form of awareness, which is not the same as our everyday, normal awareness. Hardy's awareness is found in all human beings and he believed it to be advantageous in helping human beings to survive. He described this awareness as "potential", implying that whilst it was there for all human beings, not all of us recognize or develop it.

Westerhoff says that faith is an internal, dynamic belief, while religion is the expression of that belief and that there is a clear differential between the two. He continues that faith is deeply personal, a living, growing belief; Westerhoff would say that my religion is how I express my belief held within.

The only definition in the Bible for the word "faith" is speaking of confidence and trust in the love of God, his power and his action in the world:

> *Faith is the assurance of things hoped for, the conviction of things not seen.*
>
> **Hebrews 11:1**

It is presumed that we learn our faith through religious Christian education, but it is possible to know all about God, but not to know God. It is equally true that one can teach adults and children alike about the Christian religion, but one cannot give them faith. Jesus recognized this problem when he told the parable of the sower, found in Mark 4:3-9. The story is told, the seeds are sown, but only some grow, and then some that did grow die (something we are well acquainted with in Christian education). Within the story is the hint that something deeply mystical needs to take place within the person to integrate the story so that it helps faith to develop. Our task is to sow the seed and wait for the seed to grow; the image of faith growing up with the person. So now we need to examine how the faith development theories inform our understanding of internal processes as a story is received and taken on board, internalized, to become part of ourselves and our own spirituality.

Fowler's stages of faith[1]

Stage 0: undifferentiated faith

This corresponds to the first two years. During this period, the seeds of faith are laid, in the form of trust, hope, and love, as incoming care answers a child's needs to be cared for and loved. Children who are not given enough one-to-one attention at this time will be severely damaged as individuals and less able to love in a real relationship than those whose significant others – usually parents – have met their needs for touch, contact, and love. We cannot know about the faith of such a child as there is no way that we can access their memories, but we can see the qualities that come from a good experience of this stage in life – people who possess the qualities of trust, mutuality, hope, and courage will be able to move through life in a more positive way, and their later faith development is probably more advanced. The child needs to learn a balance as to where they are in the scheme of things – to give and take in relationships, and the foundation for this quality is laid down at this stage in life. The transition to the next stage begins when thought and language begin to converge, so enabling the child to think using speech and ritualized play.

Stage 1: intuitive-projective faith/the impulse self [2]

Children at the transition to stage 1 (which is approximately two to six years) will begin to play more games where they are checking out the permanence of objects; they enjoy repeatedly naming objects. The sharing of language with others means the quality of relationship changes and small children explore the language-based world enthusiastically. The "what" and "why" questions come thick and fast and the parents may feel it will never end. The child's ability to seemingly lose interest in your answer is sometimes hard to cope with, when the interest switches immediately to something completely different, but equally important (to the child). At this stage, a child's thinking is not reversible, so they are working to a different logic to their long-suffering parents/carers; we may not be able to answer their questions appropriately because the child really does have a different agenda functioning. Critically, the child has no understanding of cause and effect. "If I do this, then that will happen" is not going on in the child's mind. Once a person has that cause and effect, we cannot think without it coming into play. Hence the difficulty of comprehension, quite apart from the child's inevitably more limited vocabulary and thinking skills.

Stage 1 children have a relatively uncontrolled imagination, where reality and fantasy blend easily. Life is episodic – one thing after another – and is very much a montage of events, which do not have a consistent narrative. Good is good and bad is bad, and the child cannot reason as an adult might. The symbols and rituals of life are deeply significant, for a child in this stage they are literally what they stand for – the child cannot discriminate as an adult might. Children learn at an amazing rate at this stage; the brain grows and develops very rapidly. The child, however, cannot discriminate between reality and fantasy as an adult does and the two exist side by side. Faith is very much an imitation of what the child experiences from adults. Images and symbols are very important to aid understanding. Whilst children in this stage may find the language of rituals in church difficult, images found in churches, such as stained-glass windows and other symbols, will feed their spirit. Stories increasingly capture the attention of the stage 1 child, with illustrations reinforcing the sense of the words. Many children in this stage will have a preferred book, which they will listen to repeatedly.

It is worth recognizing that even children from atheist homes have a clear, albeit very personal, concept of God. We each arrive at school with a clear understanding of what the word "God" means, even if our environment denies God's existence.[3]

Our task in church is to provide children with a supportive environment, in which we listen to the stories and fantasies that the child brings, not telling them what to think, but giving value to the child through our very being and the way that we interact with them.

Fairy tales hold tremendous importance for the child at this stage, helping them to work though all sorts of scenarios, many of which will never occur in the child's life, but helping them to think about the "what-ifs" of life. Bible stories such as Daniel in the lion's den, and many of Jesus' parables, will be very important to children of this age, even if they don't understand them in the way that an adult will. Many of the child's positive and negative feelings will stay with them for the rest of their life, sometimes at an unconscious level, so it is important that the language we use regarding God and faith are not the negative, judgmental words to which our parents may have been subjected. It is during this stage that many children have profound spiritual experiences, which they may now tell an adult. If they do choose to share though, it is critical that adults do not "pooh pooh" their account, but listen and accept, even if it seems far-fetched. For example, Kate Adams has researched children who say they see angels.[4] If an adults' response is "of course you haven't" this can cause existential angst in the child, who has had an extraordinary experience and is frustrated because in their eyes adults are always right. We may think the child is fantasizing, but if you share it, you'll find lots of adults saying, "Oh, so-and-so says they see angels." I once had an elderly man ask me if these angels scared the children. When I replied that I didn't know, he told me that it hadn't scared him. Children need to be taken seriously if they are to hold onto that experience, even if they are talking about something that we find hard to take literally. The work of David Hay, a reader in spiritual education at Nottingham University, implies that such experiences are more common than we might realize.

Stage 2: Mythic-literal faith/the imperial self

The transition to stage 2 begins as Piaget's "concrete operations" – see chapter 2 – begin to emerge. The child is now concerned to discover what is real and what only seems to be; bye bye, Father Christmas!

Children at this stage, usually aged from about six to twelve, have moved on to thinking skills that are based around language as well as an increasing sophistication of emotional language. The chaos of the previous stage is falling into place, with cause and effect being understood. The child now recognizes story and reality. Thought is reversible, and other perspectives can be taken on board, so their own narratives will change radically, but the child still cannot step back from their story and question it.

It is at this stage that telling our Christian stories becomes increasingly important. For stage 2 worshippers, story is one of the key ways of understanding meaning. As we work with children of this age, the potency of story and narrative is a key constituent for supporting a child's developing faith. The child will ask, "But is this real?" in response to stories such as the valley of dry bones (Ezekiel 37). (My response to that question is that it was like Ezekiel's dream.) They like their stories to have a "goody" and a "baddy", so stories such as David and Goliath, or the *Star Wars* films, will be hugely popular.

Children at this stage know that God is in charge of the world and loves each one of us. When asked about God, a child may actually come up with the old man with a beard answer. Ruby, who is eight, drew a picture of a love heart in response to what God looks like for her.[5] God is very much like a super version of a parent, but that will be affected by the home that they come from.

Children in stage 2 cannot reflect in an abstract way, so teachers may wish to note that we cannot draw out the moral at the end of a story or parable! You might like to just end a story by letting the children think about that as they go about their lives; whilst this is not "giving them the gospel", it is trusting God's Spirit, and the power of the story itself to communicate more deeply, and in the way that the child may need to hear today.

We need to recognize that some adults never move past this stage. For those who move on, puberty is the catalyst for transition.

Stage 3: synthetic-conventional faith

This stage begins to be observed as the child moves into their teenage years, with its associated self-consciousness and need to establish identity. It is accompanied by "formal operations" (see chapter 2) in their cognitive skills. The growing child's experience of the world expands rapidly with the change in schooling and the way that relationships work for the individual. Faith at this stage has to work to provide the basis for the outlook and identity of the young person.

This stage is actually where many adults rest for the remainder of their life; it is one of "conformity", of belonging to the group without questioning. The person is tuned in to the expectations and judgments of the group and is not confident enough of their own identity to question profoundly and so stand aside of the group. Beliefs and values are deeply felt, but they are not beliefs and values that the person has examined critically whilst taking them on. Authority is located in people who are perceived to be the incumbents of the tradition, for instance, in many churches, the incumbent being the vicar/rector/minister. The young person takes on their own story and holds the past in tension with an expected future.

The problems in this stage are probably occurring to you as you read; the person may give up their own judgment to the authority figure, never questioning their faith and so not being able to move into the next transition. If that authority figure is perceived to have failed the individual, they may despair of faith and lose religious faith altogether.

Transition to the next stage is indicated by the person (now a young adult) clashing with the tradition and policies of the group, which the person regards as sacrosanct, being changed (for example, a change in service from Latin to vernacular for Roman Catholics, *Book of Common Prayer* to *Common Worship* for Anglicans, gay marriage, the list is probably endless), encountering circumstances that challenge the belief system. Many people move into transition as they leave home and the security and support that "home" offers. This move from security into a more challenging world enables the young adult to question their faith, which may have not been developing for some time.[6]

Fowler himself points out that to move from stage 3 onwards requires a certain level of education and articulation. If a person only achieves a minimal level of education, they will not achieve Piaget's "formal operations" (see chapter 2) and will not be able to move beyond stage 3 faith. Stage 4 requires the ability to think in the abstract, to reason and use logic. This again underlines the importance of our use of language to encourage children to widen their understanding and vocabulary and work towards formal operations.

Fowler states that for faith to grow and develop, we must let go of our previous images – we have to go through a short, or sometimes not so short, period of doubt and questioning. An image I find useful is that of a jigsaw puzzle. When completed, you clearly see the image. However, when you reach a transition period in faith development, someone has thrown your jigsaw up in the air and it's come down in lots of pieces. As you progress through the transition, the puzzle pieces are re-assembled, but when you finish the transition, arriving at the next stage, you discover that actually the image on the puzzle has changed slightly, or even quite substantively.

Fowler's theory goes beyond this stage, through to the end of life, but you will need to read another book to find out the next episode as it is beyond the brief for a book on the spirituality of children and young people.

Westerhoff's theory of faith development

Alongside Fowler's theory of faith development, we also need to be aware of that developed by John Westerhoff.[7]

Westerhoff recognizes Fowler's work, but has devised his own system of faith development, which is quite different. Westerhoff says faith is an action, a verb. It results from our actions with others, changing and expanding through these actions, expressing itself through them. So Westerhoff places faith entirely within a community of faith – it is not possible to be a person of faith who lives in isolation. Westerhoff speaks of faith with a religious subtext, whereas Fowler believes people of no religious persuasion, as well as those who have religious persuasion, may have faith.

Westerhoff sees faith very much along the lines of a tree, growing and spreading, where faith is the equivalent of the rings found inside the bark. He proposes four styles of faith rather than stages, and each grows around the previous style, or ring. Therefore, the person who has moved right through faith, and has moved to the fourth style, has within them the previous three, and needs to attend to the needs of all four styles of faith. Indeed, if the needs of a "previous", deeper, buried style of faith are not being met, the person will defer back to the earlier style and meet the needs of that before returning to the more recent style of faith.

This is a clear difference with Fowler, who proposes that a person "leaves" each stage as they move through life. Both Fowler and Westerhoff insist that there is no "pecking order" of faith – that no style is in any way "superior" or "better than" any other, it's simply where you are at the present time. But it is difficult to read Fowler without feeling that he sees the later stages of faith as movement and progress, rather as a PhD is better than a BA, or as A levels are better than GCSEs. He seems to see life as a progress towards stage 6. Westerhoff has a more egalitarian feel to his theory.

Westerhoff believes that faith will only grow if given the right environment, that it is possible to arrest faith development by not giving it the right conditions for growth, just as trees will stop growing if there is a drought, they become pot-bound, or the soil does not contain the right nutrients. He points out that this is still a complete tree, it's just not growing or developing anymore. Westerhoff stresses that we need interaction with other people of faith if we are to grow and develop. Faith is an action that includes thinking, feeling, and willing. It is transmitted, sustained, and expanded through our interactions with other people of faith in community. These interactions are the nutrients and water that keep the tree of faith growing and developing.

Trees grow slowly, very slowly in most cases. We don't notice them growing, and faith is like this. We may suddenly notice a change, just as my children always seemed to grow overnight, and I only noticed the growth as we said our "goodbye" in the morning and stood next to one other. So we don't see the growth in faith slowly taking place, but we will notice the result. Growth like this cannot be forced or rushed, we can just be with people as they slowly move from one style of faith further out, making the new ring as they take on a new style of faith.

Style one: experienced faith

Experienced faith results from interactions with others of faith. No one can determine another's faith, or give another faith, but we share our lives and faith with one another. Others do the same and through this mutual giving and receiving we sustain and transmit and expand our faith. This is the style of faith of the preschool and early childhood years, where faith is experienced through action and interaction. All children initiate action and respond to actions of others; a child will explore and test, imagine and create, experience and react in their day-to-day lives. This is how they learn – from putting food into their mouth to find out if they like it, and it's good, to responding to the love and care of their parents and carers. A child's actions influence those with whom they interact – a laugh or a disgruntled noise will illicit very different responses. The actions of others will affect and influence them. Their acts prove a mirror and test for those whom they interact with – we all recognize the scenario where children push things to the limit to discover where the boundaries are, or where they need to draw out precisely what the ground rules are; children can live with different rules in different places easily and with no seeming effort once the rules have been explained. They take off shoes as they enter one friend's house, while at another house they walk mud all over the new cream carpet!

The characteristics of this type of faith continue for us all and are foundational to all people's faith. For example, we all need to be hugged – it is easy with children but more difficult with teenagers or adults. We all need to continue to act in ways that explore and test, imagine and create, experience and react. We continue to learn as we meet new people, develop new relationships, and engage in new patterns of working and being.

For all people, experiences relating to words are more important than the words themselves. You can say you love me, but I'll expect you to act in that way too, or I'll soon think I can't take you at your word. Our language and experience are interrelated to the point where we find it difficult to think of one without the other – we think about our experiences in language after all. The three most important experiences are trust, love, and acceptance for Christians and this need continues throughout life. We should be "doers of the word, and not merely hearers" (James 1:22). People who do not act as Christians are soon recognized by those outside the community of faith, who will quickly level the accusation of hypocrisy.

Thus, for this style of faith to flourish, we need to provide an environment of sharing and interaction between people of faith. We all need to be Christian with others, all of the time.

Style two: affiliative faith

If we could model experienced faith as two people looking up and down, or as a child holding an adult's hand, this style of faith is much more egalitarian – two people facing each other, or two people of the same age holding hands, walking side by side.

This style comes after successful experienced faith and builds upon that style. Style two is all about acting with others in an accepting community with a clear sense of identity. We all need to belong to a self-conscious community, able to actively participate and share in its life and in a church community this is often seen through people joining the choir or the youth club, or acting as sides-people/stewards at worship services. We all have a need to feel wanted and needed, to be missed when not we're not there, and to contribute to the whole.

This is a period of religious affections and heartfelt belief; a person's intuitional way of being there is as important as the intellectual – I need to feel my faith as much as I think about my faith. Thus you see people participating in the arts – drama, music, dance, painting and so forth – and this involvement is critical for working out the emotional attachment to the faith as well as Bible reading reflecting the thinking through of faith.

Authority is found in the community's communication of a story and way of life that judges and inspires actions. So the teaching of the faith through formal situations is primal for the person in this style of faith.

Style two faith is first experienced through action, then secondly experienced through images and story. Thus there is the need to learn the community's story, and to internalize, rehearse, and personally own the story that undergirds the community's faith. This again is done through the formal teaching of the community – Sunday school or sermon, Bible class or youth club quiet times.

Typically, this is the faith of the young teenager, as they begin to take on the responsible roles of the community, and so become integrated into adult membership of the group.[8]

Recent developments

More recently, Westerhoff has changed the model that he uses to describe faith development to that of a journey. He states that all faith begins in an experience of nature and that we enter the faith journey through one of two ways: either through an experiential route – learning faith in community, symbols, sacred stories, and rituals, which he calls "affective", or through a reflective route – making sense of life through their own experiences, which Westerhoff calls "intellectual".

Less frequently, people grow in faith through the "integrative" path, where they discern the truth from a combination of the other two. As you travel through life, you will have various accompaniers, who travel with you for a time before you separate, but with time both intellectual and affective streams will come together towards a holistic faith, incorporating heart and head knowledge. Some fortunate people enter the journey with the two streams already balanced, but most of us enter through the one which we habitually use – a bit like the right brain/left brain idea. This also makes sense within the context of the spiritual styles theory (see chapter 4).

So now, for Westerhoff, faith is seen as a journey, in which you must be accompanied by other people of faith, all seeking the truth.

Both Fowler and Westerhoff first published these theories in the 1980s. This latest addition to Westerhoff's theory is found in the 2012 edition of *Will Our Children Have Faith*.[9] It is clearly influenced by the thinking that the mushrooming interest in children's spirituality of the last twenty years has brought about, especially that of David Csinos and his theory of spiritual styles.[10]

Sarah Brush

Sarah Brush, working in the 2010s, brings a new, fresh eye to the debate. She also sees faith development in the metaphor of a growing tree, but while Westerhoff looks at the rings of the tree, she uses the stages of a tree's life, from seed to seedling to sapling to maturity to totem. She points out that seedlings may not look like the mature tree, and how carefully they need to be nurtured if we want them to thrive. Transplanting seedlings is a risky business, but with the right conditions the seedling will grow to be a sapling. Staking young trees is common, but if the staking is not done with care, the tree will become deformed and unhealthy, and the sapling still needs much attention. In all three conditions, the young tree needs the right conditions both above and below the surface if growth is to be healthy. She also looks at the effects of the seasons on a tree – how rapid growth in the spring becomes fruiting in the summer, with leaf loss in autumn, and very little, if any, signs of life in winter. This reflects well on how people's faith may indeed grow in "fits and starts", with most of us going through the dark winter nights of the soul to emerge with fresh growth – very much picking up on Fowler's stage 4 of existential doubts. As the sapling becomes a mature tree the rapid growth slows down and the tree becomes quite different – solid and firm, bending in the wind, occasionally losing branches but fruiting generously. As the tree ages, so it may seem to die, but it will still harbour life such as birds and insects, and eventually the fungi and moulds take over as the tree breaks down to feed the next generation. She refers to this dying tree as a totem – a sign of wisdom from years of life that is now being given to the next generation, and those that are to follow.

The great insight that Brush brings for children and youth ministers is that of the need for the sapling to be tended to at a distance. It needs to be itself. Autumn and winter will be hard, as it won't be strong enough to survive difficult conditions, but then spring comes and life surges through, with growth and flowering once again. It's OK to have fallow periods, and indeed, we should expect them. Brush also recognizes that many acorns never become oak trees, but who knows what is happening in the hearts of those young people for whom growth in faith seems to have stalled?

Growth tree
Two modes of change and progression combined

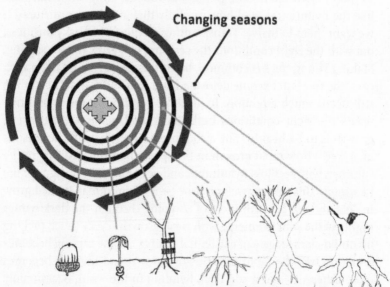

Changing seasons

© S. Brush, 2019   **1. Seed   2. Seedling   3. Sapling   4. Young Tree   5. Mature Tree   6. Totem**

Sandy Eisenberg Sasso

Sandy Eisenberg Sasso comes to the debate with the wisdom of rabbinic teaching. She believes that we grow through a cycle of "experience" followed by "contextualizing the story", culminating in our "theology". For example, I might feel close to God looking up at the stars. By telling someone else about that experience it becomes more real for me, and I can begin to think in different ways about the experience – what can I learn, how can I remember and share this? Thus the experience may come to underpin my personal theology and then begin to effect change in the community of faith that I belong to. The ultimate example for Christians must be that of Communion; a group meets to share their stories of Jesus, which over the years becomes a liturgy as they practise the story, until it's a bedrock of Christian theology. As those who minister, we need to have a library of stories, including our own personal story, that we share in response to questions about faith, which hold within them the power of myth – they are not necessarily true, but they hold truth. The stories need to be well told and in appropriate language – not simplistic or childish, but child friendly and rich in metaphor. Sasso is a skilled writer of such stories, which explore various existential questions in a layered and subtle way, with beautiful illustrations.

Godly Play (see chapter 8) is possibly the best story telling method for this – the wondering at the end places the listener within the story, each in their own place. It can be revisited over and over as we grow in years, and the meaning of the story will grow and change as we do. Thus our personal faith, our theology in practice, is individual – always true, but more overt in this cyclical theory. Sasso believes that as we experience story, so we add to our theology after reflecting and dwelling on the story. Each person's theology will reflect where they grew up, how they grew up, and will be coloured by their personal experience.

Doubt

So what is the place of doubt in the lives of all people of faith?

If we are acquainted with the theories of faith development, then we see doubt as part of the journey of faith. It is normal and desirable and part of the child becoming an adult – it means that we have tussled with the questions that occur as we grow older and our experience of life widens, and we come to our own understanding – an owned faith rather than a learned faith. And if our faith keeps changing as the theories suggest, doubt gives us a foundation from which we can engage with the difficulties that we all have as we travel through life in a more reasoned and adult manner. Brush's theory of the seasons is especially helpful and reassuring as we consider the place of doubt and times when God seems far away – we are in the winter season, the "dark night of the soul", but she assures us that, given time, spring will return, with the promise of new growth. Critically, it is after the fallow season that trees change shape and may not be recognized as the sapling of last year. As ministers, it is our responsibility to be stakes to these growing trees and allow them to become the tree that they were born to be. Often that is more about being there than having the answers.

The children and young people that we work with within the scope of the church's mission are all found somewhere on the continuums described above. There will be some that Fowler's scheme seems to describe better than Westerhoff, and there will be others for whom Westerhoff seems to have the fit far more accurately. There will be others who play out Sasso's theory clearly, others for whom Brush's metaphor makes most sense. The schemes are simply tools to help us to understand what is going on as we all develop and grow in our faith as human beings. The crux is to be able to stand with our children and young people as they grow and develop, to nurture and encourage them as they grow towards the integrity of person that faith offers. If understanding these theories of how people grow enables me to be there more fully for those with whom I have been entrusted, then it was worth the reading and thinking.

Questions for discussion

1. Which of these schemes do you prefer? Can you say why?

2. What is your practice with children and young people who ask challenging questions?

3. Where do you find yourself in these schemes?

CHAPTER 7

The story so far

Amy looked up at the bright shining sun. "Hello Grandad,"
she said.
Amy, five years old

You've probably worked your way through the first few chapters of this book wondering just how all these different theories apply to you as you teach children and young people week by week. What we need to do now is to stick them all together, to overlay the differing theories to see what they can tell us about children and young people at different stages of development. This should give us a way in to understand the different, and sometimes very strange, behaviours that we see in our children and young people.

Let's begin where we begin, in church, with children who are in what we could call early childhood – children from about two to six years old. Younger children are not usually in a special group in a church context, other than a crèche, and there we encourage healthy play and activity, using the many toys available (and usually donated!).

Children from about two years upwards are in the stage that Piaget called **preoperational** or **intuitive.** These are children who are brimming with imagination and creativity. They see the world very much from their own perspective and cannot see it from another's point of view. These are the children who don't understand conservation – remember the illustration about juice in a glass? They are still learning how to behave in a social setting, so our children will, from time to time, get it seriously wrong and we need to support and encourage them as they learn socialization skills. Our primary school classes have "the carpet" area in their rooms and children respond well to that defined area, learning to sit quietly, listening to whoever is speaking, and indicating by putting up their hand or some other technique that they wish to contribute to the discussion. (An effective trick is to throw a small cuddly toy to the child who can speak, always via the teacher, who says, "You can only speak if you're holding Patch/Rover/Bouncer." Try it – it works well with five-to seven-year olds,)

Children from two years will mirror other children's behaviour – so if one child laughs out loud, chances are that the others will too, sometimes making a horrible forced laugh sound, as they join in with a joke they may not have understood, wanting to be part of the larger group. Children coming into this stage will still throw tantrums (so do some adults, but that's another subject), but as they move through this stage they come to realize that they cannot always have their own way, especially if they are well handled. More importantly, they come to realize that there is more than one way and begin to be able to take that on board.

From Erikson's point of view, there are two stages during this period. First comes **autonomy versus shame,** a period of increasing independence from the child's carer; toilet training and other forms of independence, such as learning how to eat with cutlery, are still going on, and how far the child progresses will depend on their motor skills – and this is incredibly variable. Using a knife and fork is a very complicated skill, but to those of us who do it all the time it is very important that we are supportive of children as they tackle these skills. Watching children colour, do a jigsaw, and other hand-eye co-ordinated tasks shows us how different children of this age can be, and gives a pretty good indication of how manually dextrous the child will be when grown up. Even doing up shoes with Velcro fasteners is a challenge for some children of this age. Don't assume!

Once the child has reached about four to five years, they will enter the stage called **initiative versus guilt.** You will see this as the child begins to organize games; rules and regulations become more important. Friendships become mutual. Learning is accelerating as the child "mops up" whatever they can.

In Fowler's scheme of faith development, the child will be in the **intuitive-projective faith/the impulse self** stage. As the child explores language, laying down the enormous bank of words that stand for various concepts, they will chatter and query sometimes non-stop. It's important for us to remember that this child does not have reversible thinking – they really can't flip ideas around as adults do, so we need to keep our expectations realistic. The child lives in a world where one thing follows another – it's a straight line and there is no understanding of the subtle shades of grey that most adults use when reasoning. Someone is either a "goody" or a "baddy", but we understand that sometimes something fantastic takes place and the baddy becomes good. Symbols and rituals are very important, so don't forget to sing "Happy Birthday", or do a proper nativity play! Some children of this age will love to look in church buildings at the significant pieces of architecture as they cement their present understanding of faith. Children at this age do not have their own concept of faith but have acquired a kind of second-hand version from the adults with whom they share their lives. At this point, it is very important to allow space for the child to take part in the rites and rituals of church.[1] They may not understand, but that understanding will develop and grow. Story becomes increasingly important at this time; both secular and sacred stories will take up a lot of time for this child. Watch them acting out their favourite stories in the playground and at church. The Old Testament in particular will score highly, with baddies such as Goliath and goodies such as David feeding the child's imagination and understanding.

Westerhoff places children's faith right through to adolescence as **experienced faith.** A child's faith at this stage is a reflection of the faith that they experience from other people; through a child's experimentation and interaction with the world, they will develop and grow in their faith. If adults are kind, patient, and accepting of a child, then they will associate this with church, faith, and being a Christian. I don't need to spell out the corollary. They see people's reactions to them as a mirror of themselves, and they need to have rules and boundaries clearly defined and adhered to in church as well as at home. Westerhoff's model requires people to be clearly

Christian in every area of their lives if our children are to grow and develop in faith. Brush speaks of the tiny sapling, and how important it is to care for this delicate plant, as faith at this stage could indeed be stamped out by excluding a child or behaving in ways that do not support and nurture their spirituality. And a child's spirituality is far more inclusive that that of many adults.

At this stage a child is highly susceptible to our view of God, so we need to ensure that what we teach about God is reflecting a biblical, loving perspective, not overlaid with our own personal hang-ups. Research into the different generations explores how those of different ages may hold a very different model of God, but how often do we actually share at this level and check that my model of God is the same as yours? Likewise, the model of God that our children will hold when they are older may well depend on their experience of the faith community when they are children.[2]

In my daily work, I come across people who in their deep beliefs have a very fierce model of God. This is often communicated by their worry about a deceased loved one and "where they are now". People with this view of a judgmental God frequently fear that because the person was not a confessing Christian they have not gone to heaven. They tend to be older, coming from a generation that heard sermons about hell and damnation rather more than my own flocks of the past, but this model of God is deeply imprinted within their psyche, giving a God who is demanding and people who are fearful of committing mortal sin every time they do anything tending towards the fun/risky/dubious. This is the generation that will be grandparents/great-grandparents and these are often the people who are the practising Christians in today's society. This makes the example that the children receive from the adults at church very important – we need to be always aware of the model of God that we have uppermost within our own understanding. Using a good teaching scheme will help here as it will give guidelines as to how to effectively interact with the children. Be aware that children who have suffered abuse of any type will have a damaged model of what a parent is like, and sadly it's frequently fathers who come out worst here, so do try to have mixed gender adults with your class and be conscious of the modelling that is going on through the way that adults interact with each other, so that damaged children come to see that there is a different way of relating; one that is more like our heavenly Father.

For many churches, there is little problem with children of this age, as they may well be shunted out of the worshipping centre and into another room to "play". Modern thinking questions the value of this, other than removing sources of noise from the adults. It is costly on the parents, but I would now encourage parents to keep their children with them in church for as much of the time as possible, quietly explaining what is going on with the child, but also using books and quiet toys for when the attention span expires. Children learn by watching adults.

From about six, children move on for all three models. Piaget calls his next stage **concrete operations.** Logical thinking is beginning to occur, reading is enabling children to feed their imaginations through their own choice of materials and resources, and they have developed the ability to take a concrete object and draw from it a generalization. So, for example, we can group some stories and call them "parables". Bible stories are enjoyed more and more, and children of this age will enjoy learning facts and figures, so it's good to use these in our teaching.

Erikson's name for this stage is **industry versus inferiority.** This is the stage where the child absorbs the cultural norms of their society, so worship and interior life needs to be reflected in the home. Children at this stage like to make things, so encourage the children in your care to do so – think of all those worksheets that the Sunday school materials provide! Now give the children permission to ignore them if they fancy doing something a bit more creative or spontaneous. Let them make their own Christingles and Easter gardens, let them paint and engage with lots of different craft activities. As the name "industry versus inferiority" implies, they continue to need positive reinforcement, carrots rather than sticks, in their lives. At present, the morality of the reality TV show is prevalent in many children's lives and this often comes with quite appalling treatment of people as the norm. Again, modelling Christ-like attitudes, questioning these norms and being like Christ to the children will help them to question those norms of society around us. This is, of course, laying enormous responsibility at the feet of the adults who minister with our children and this should be acknowledged and honoured within the church. Ensuring that the carrots are non-material is also important in this time of cash-rich time-poor parents. Some of these children are bought off all too often – if the reward is quality time, then that is a true reward. In Fowler's scheme, we now come to **mythic-literal faith/the imperial self.** This can be a tricky stage to work with children as they will begin to question "But is it real, is it true?" They don't have, as yet, the sophisticated thinking processes that allows them to understand "what is truth" and the complex thinking around literal and metaphorical truth, but we need to be there to help them to work on it. Story continues to be critical at this stage as they work on their own role in the faith story that they are part of. Their thinking is reversible and they can begin to understand someone else's point of view, so they will ask increasingly sophisticated questions. We need to remember their inability to take a moral from a story. Teachers at school (like some preachers in church) will be used to telling the children "what the story means today" but I suggest you stop! Simply tell the story and then ask the children to think about it during the day and see what they think it's all about. It's a bit scary as a learning technique as we have to trust the child, and the Holy Spirit, to work together towards what the story really said to them, and that may be quite incomprehensible to us as adults! Stage 2 "faithers" like to be given rules and regulations, know their boundaries, and learn what is right and what is wrong. It is during the next stage that the big questions will be asked.

The main thing to remember with all these levels is that the children do not have the power of abstract thinking (neither do some adults). So, we need to keep our lessons concrete based, using lots of visual materials, and allowing the child to re-work the story afterwards.

Thus we come to the big one – adolescence! This stage begins once a child starts to become self-conscious and self-aware in a new way. You know what I mean. However, and this is very important, if a child has built up a real and good working relationship with the adults they meet in church, they can be very important to that child as they become a young person and are inevitably in conflict with their parents/carers from time to time.

Piaget defines this stage as **formal operations** and this stage continues into adulthood. The key point is the beginning of abstract thought and the self-consciousness that brings a developing young adult to a whole new way of relating. Peer groups become very important, and if they are moving in a group outside of Christianity and the church, it becomes increasingly hard for them to stay with us at this time. One of our older boy choristers in my last parish was recently caught seriously on the back foot when one of his (male) school friends appeared in the congregation. By the time we got to the end of the service he'd come up with the ultimate reason for being in a church choir – "just look at all those girls!" he declared to his suddenly very envious friend. There were indeed three girls to every boy!

Erikson names this phase **identity versus role confusion** and this sums up a great deal for how many of us see adolescence. We should never underestimate how hard this stage can be for our young people as they develop their own personalities and decide who they really are as opposed to who their family/carers wish them to be. We all know about door slamming, summed up brilliantly in the Harry Enfield character "Kevin". Indeed, we sometimes called our own children Kevin when they were a bit out of line (as if!). It worked very well. Using the language of comedy characters helps our young people to know that we have some awareness of their world, although us oldies have to guard against being too trendy – there is a need to break away and for us to recognize we aren't the same age and we don't have the same pressures. And there is nothing as cringe-inducing as an adult trying to be "down with the kids". Act your age and be genuine. For us in church, this is a very threatening stage, as young people leave church rapidly at this age, or they grasp their faith hard and hold tight to their childish faith as if it's a protection against the storm that they are living through.

Fowler calls this stage of faith **synthetic-conventional faith.** Faith at this stage has to work to provide the basis for the outlook and identity of the young person. They are well tuned into conformity at this point and they will sometimes trim their thinking to fit in with what they experience around them. They need to feel that they are part of a group, so Sunday schools who have a larger group for young teenagers will now call it by a different name, such as "Pathfinders", and chances are it will have a more youth club feel, perhaps with an evening meeting. Relationships between the young people are incredibly important, and rows can be vicious and stormy, but brief and quickly overcome. The authority figure for the young person is critical. They may well absolutely believe them, which is scary for you if you are cast in this role. The young person will possibly stay in this stage for the rest of their life, moving through adulthood by not attending to the existential questions that occur or by belonging to a church that is more authoritarian in its style.

There may come a point where the young person, usually about eighteen by now, begins to ask questions of their assumed faith to which the only answer is outside of Christian faith as far they can see. This usually comes with the big move away from home, especially if they go to university, and out of the real sphere of influence of their parents/carers.[3] It is vital that the adults stay in touch with these young people, affirming them as they struggle with their faith as they move through stage 4, so that they arrive at the position that is their own, owned faith and one that is open to question. Many people are lost to the church at this time, but they are frequently the ones who come back once they are parents themselves – so don't despair. My own feeling is that it's more important for our young people to leave the church and struggle to find their own faith than to stay in the church with a childish faith that is not robust and able to engage in dialogue with the world in which they move.

According to Westerhoff, if a child has a successful experience of experienced faith, then as they enter adolescence their faith will move into the **affiliative faith** style. This is about belonging, with the importance already seen of peer groups, helping in church with various tasks, being seen to be a real member. If we are feeling brave, by looking at these young people as they move towards adulthood, the health of their faith will give us an idea of how we have been communicating our faith and sharing with them. As the young person's emotional life becomes more reflective, the opportunity to join in with drama, music, and the arts around church enables them to "feel" their faith as well as think it. This is particularly important and quite challenging for people whose personality is more intellectually than intuitively based. The growing person needs to learn the story of their own faith, and the story of this particular community of faith, so times spent together reflecting on the shared journey will be of benefit to all.

It is during adolescence that we see personality traits firming up, as the introverts and extroverts become more so and learning styles become more obvious. Personality is never set, but the stronger, dominant traits are becoming more accentuated at this time.

Our response

So how do we respond to these changes and needs within the church? Firstly, it is important that the needs of children and young people at different stages are catered for, and this means that the model you use needs to be fluid as children of different stages and ages pass through your group. Inevitably, many Sunday school teachers are there because their children and young people are seen as learners. This is great as it often means the parents are learning about the Christian faith alongside their children, and they are also well aware of what their children can and cannot manage. The problem comes if they forget what their children were like as they grew older, and the group can become targeted towards a very defined group of children and their particular needs. So, ideally, you do need to have someone there who does not have a familial tie to a particular child or group.

The terms Key Stage 1 (Infants) and Key Stage 2 (Juniors) used by schools may have been arrived at accidentally, but as we've seen there is a sense of breaking the group at about six years, as faith and cognitive and personality development all go through a change at this point. Clearly, after adolescence hits, you will need to radically change the provision for any young people who are still with you. They may join the team as "junior leaders", or they may choose to go and sit in with the adults. Children who joined the church choir at about seven, who wish to leave the choir (boys especially, as their voices break), may find it very hard to sit with the rest of the congregation, so consider a special role for these young people (we tried to recruit them as servers, but that's very Anglican/Roman Catholic).

The various schemes and materials that are on the market vary enormously, and you will have found the scheme that suits your church, but I would encourage you to look at the next chapter on Godly Play and think about incorporating different storytelling styles in your group. Buy more schemes than the one you habitually use and cannibalize the best bits into your regular scheme; variety is the spice of life.

Consider how you begin your week-by-week sessions; do you have a quiet start or a noisy one? When I started in my present post, we had a stunningly talented young man who started the week's session with dancing, doing actions to Christian songs in a way that I had never seen before (or since). The children adored this young man (who is now a professional puppeteer) and would hurtle in through the doors! They then had a quiet "down" time incorporated into the session so that everyone could get their breath back! After this young man left us for gainful employment (and how we missed him!) we developed a quiet, colouring time during the children's arrival. This has now become singing songs to a newer teacher's guitar playing. So use what you've got and aim for a start that uses the talents you have and the children and young people who are attending. Both the dancing and the singing starts suit more extrovert, emotion spiritual style children more than the more sensitive, shy children. If we encourage parents to stay with their children for the first few sessions, we rely on the parents to help their children join this noisier activity, or to look at the books that are always available in the quiet corner of the room.

As you move into the story time, let all your teachers tell the story. Everyone will have a different style, and variety is good. Variety in your response time, be it doing drama, crafts, or other responses, is critical. Children and young people like to know the structure and what will happen within a broad-brush outline, but will become bored if every week is effectively the same.

Never forget the importance of language – language and vocabulary are the building bricks of the child's understanding of God, their faith, and their spirituality. Without the right vocabulary the children and young people cannot understand. So ensure that your storytelling uses the right words. Children are used to jargon and technical language. I recently entered a year five class (nine and ten-year-olds) and they were learning about metaphors and similes. I still can't remember which is which, but at eleven we expect our children to, and many do. So don't underestimate the blotting paper nature of a child's ability to learn new, correct words and use them.

I would encourage you to increasingly involve all young people in the tasks of church, perhaps convening a junior PCC/church committee, so that they have a chance to speak and be heard.[4] Use them as stewards/sides-people. They are often better readers than all those adults who dominate the reading rota. Why can't they lead the prayers? How about taking the collection? The more they are used for perceived adult roles, the more they will feel that we are taking them seriously as committed members of the church. And don't forget that the older children may be listening to sermons now – let them have a chance to discuss them with the preacher. They often have far more questions that the adults in the congregation, who aren't usually working out their own faiths with anything like the commitment or drive. If primary-aged children can lead and plan the worship in school, why aren't they doing the same in church?

Plan well together, socialize together, and enjoy each other's contributions. Most Sunday school groups have a named leader and it is important that that role is time defined. After a few years, this person may well want a rest, even if that rest is becoming one of the regular helpers (as long as they don't try to take that authority back).

There is also the question of boundaries – and of following good safeguarding practice – which, in a social media world, need to be drawn. Is it a good idea for your young people's leader to be friends with everyone they minister with on Facebook? A closed account for the group makes more sense, but you'll need to explain the choices going on to the group. Likewise with Instagram and other sites – does everyone agree to having their image online, even in a closed group? I get angry when I find my image posted without prior permission, but few people seem to understand why. So this is something to be debated in your meetings, and then expect everyone to stick to the rules. In the same way, if you employ a special minister for this area, they need to leave the church Facebook page closed and avoid work-related social media on their day off, as well as guarding their privacy for the sake of their sanity and their family life.

Questions for discussion

1. How challenging do you find this consideration of different theories of child development? Have you considered these theories before?

2. How does your group need to adjust its working to include an awareness of children who develop differently?

3. What are your social media boundaries?

4. What represents the biggest challenge to you personally in this chapter?

CHAPTER 8

Godly Play

*We were attending a very high church, where the priest
held a piece of the consecrated bread in his fingers as he
blessed children on the head. When we got back to our pew,
Jim turned and said, "You got yours in your mouth, but I
got mine through my head."*

Jim, three years old

In this chapter I want to briefly examine the system of Christian
education called "Godly Play" through an overview of its
development and a description of how a Godly Play session is run.

Open and closed learning

The English educational system works in a rather measured way.
Children are tested and their and ability is measured as they
progress through from the youngest children at nursery through
to graduation. The emphasis in school over the last decade or so
has become very much a question of learning concepts and being
able to prove that the child has done so. More people have begun to
question the actual process of learning that goes on in our schools.
While those who used to do this tended to concentrate on the mind,
the spiritual has become more important over the last decade. Now,
Ofsted[1] are inspecting for spiritual learning, and many schools are
aware, especially with the rise in recorded mental health issues
for young people, of the importance of a more holistic view of the
child/young person within the educational system.

The Christian education of children has followed the secular
trend; success for a Sunday school teacher may be a verbal
discussion that demonstrates how much of the story the children
can remember and what it means. Most Sunday teaching materials
guide teachers towards the telling of the story, some interactive

recall of the story, craftwork, and possibly a worksheet, with the child being guided clearly along the pattern for the session. Echoing secular education, we could say that many such systems have "learning objectives", even if that isn't the language used. Such methods are good for both teachers and students in that they give security and given outcomes and mimic the system that the child will know from school, but it may limit children and young people from questioning and wondering about issues that the story has aroused for them. It is described as a closed system of learning; it follows a clear path, from beginning to end, and "sidetracking" by children can be regarded as interruption rather than a real request to let the process develop in a new direction.

The process we experience in much Christian education has been described, rather negatively, as "sacred babysitting".[2] Many adults in our churches want exactly that – for the children and young people to be outside of the "main" worship, being kept busy and learning the Christian faith. And the quieter the better![3]

Open and closed questions

Much of the teaching in school is in the form of question and answers. Teachers do this because it keeps the children concentrating and they can check whether they are keeping up with the flow of information/subject matter as the lesson proceeds. If the teacher senses a child's attention wandering, they can bring them back by a question to check whether that child is "with us". If the questions can be answered with a "yes" or "no", or a very brief answer, then that question is defined as closed. So, in maths, if I ask "what's two plus two?" there is only one answer that is correct. Likewise, in science I may ask a child what their thermometer is reading as water boils, and the answer will be in the region of 100 degrees Celsius. Closed questions tend to be right or wrong, and are usually to do with learning information and facts.

If I ask a child a question about a poem, such as, "What do you think the child is feeling at this point?" the child could say all sorts of things, and each would be right. The child could say a few words, or lots, and again, either is right. This is an open question, which is asking someone to be expansive, to elucidate their personal feelings or beliefs, and has no right or wrong answer. Open questions tend to be used to get children to express their own ideas. Open questions are designed to open up thinking, rather than funnel it into a particular way of thinking, or a particular piece of knowledge.

Both types of question have their uses, but in religious education we want to be using more open questions than closed – we want to enable children to work at their own spirituality rather than give them a watered-down version of our own.

The process of Christian education

Christian educators easily fall into the trap of equating knowledge with faith. (This especially appeals to those who are Word style predominant, as they put a high value of knowledge leading to faith, and these people naturally gather within the more evangelical tradition of the church). We have already noticed that knowing about God is not the same as knowing God. We can teach children the Bible so that they can recite it from beginning to end without them experiencing anything spiritual in that recitation. Theology graduates may describe themselves as atheist. What we are about is helping children to make sense of the world from a spiritual standpoint. Knowing the story is not the same as being part of the story – as the epistle of James says, "Be doers of the word, and not merely hearers" (1:22). But who decides what a story means? How does the listener hear the story and process it in such a way that the story is internalized, that it enters their very being, their make-up as a person, and is recognized as part of their life, of their own story? Preachers and teachers tell the story and expand it, but perhaps starting from the impact that the story has had on them. The assumption is made that the listeners are following the story in the same way as the person teaching, but this cannot be supposed. Every listener brings a different experience of life, and every listener thinks in a different way from everyone else. The story will impact on every listener in a different way, and it would be good practice to encourage listeners and teachers alike to recognize this and then work with the story as is best for them, indeed, as the Spirit leads. This is a far more open way to approach the story. Recognition of the superiority of this method of sharing sacred stories is reflected in the increase in the storytelling style of a sermon, where the ends are left open, with the individual person having "arrived" in the narrative, working through the narrative as the story speaks to them.

If a person is to enter into a story there has to be an element of giving up control. They then actively live within the story's time and space while the story is being communicated through its telling. This stirs the imagination in a more creative way as the story will enter into the right side of the brain, where emotion and sensing take place. Ideally the storytelling is an interpersonal telling, with the listeners responding and the teller responding in turn to the listeners. A chorus or words that repeat are an ideal way to affect this type of telling. In the book of Daniel in the Old Testament, there are many stories where there is a chorus line. The one I like the best is the story of the golden statue, leading into the fiery furnace. King Nebuchadnezzar made a huge statue and set it up for everyone to worship him, including "the satraps, the prefects, and the governors, the counselors, the treasurers, the justices, the magistrates, and all the officials of the provinces" (Daniel 3:2-3).

There is a musical accompaniment to the worship, and that acts as a call to worship: "the sound of the horn, pipe, lyre, trigon, harp, drum, and entire musical ensemble: (3:5, 7, 15)."[4]

Look at the word-by-word repeats! Children, and adults, listening to this story would have all joined in on these – to us – crazy repeating lists. There is little as effective in keeping people's attention in a story (or a song/hymn) as repeating choruses that we all join in with.

So, we need to give our listeners the chance to participate fully, to experience open rather than closed learning, with open rather than closed questions being employed. This challenges our teaching methods, implying that there might be other ways to teach which would facilitate more open learning, and perhaps enabling children to make more sense of the spiritual world in which they live.

Development of Godly Play

Through the second half of the last century, people concerned for the spiritual growth of children worked to devise a new way of telling stories; of sharing and nurturing a child's spiritual life, rather than imposing an adult model. One of the outcomes of this work is a method of storytelling and interaction with children which is called "Godly Play". Godly Play is concerned with religious growth and how to foster it. Jerome Berryman, in his book entitled *Godly Play* explains the method in great detail, but the emphasis all through this method is in helping children to understand religious language and to use it in a creative and liberating manner.[5] Godly Play takes seriously the idea that without appropriate language we cannot grow in our spiritual understanding of the world, and aims to give us the language to do the work that needs to be done if adults are to understand their faith as clearly as a doctor might understand physiology. Without religious language we cannot make sense of our spiritual nature as we don't have the language to develop the concepts internally. Godly Play is designed to aid the use of religious language by the individual, within the context of carefully structured sessions.

At first glance, the Godly Play process does not seem as structured as many Sunday school lessons are, nor are the learning outcomes explicit, although there are very clear outcomes for those of us involved in this process. This is about teaching children how to enter into the divine game of life. But the structure has been carefully devised down through years of experimental research and testing to facilitate open learning. From the design of the learning environment, through to the pattern of the session, scrupulous thought has gone into the total experience that the children share with their teachers.

The Godly Play Session

Entering

The room the children come in to has been designed and laid out to facilitate indirect learning.[6][7] The full Godly Play classroom may not be available for all – few church groups can dedicate a room solely "Godly Play use" but if you do have such a room, the layout draws the children into the essence of the open style of learning and reflects all sorts of non-verbal messages for the learners, from the respect, equality, and learning stance of both adults and children to physical commodities such as the materials for the lessons, based around the church year and its seasons. Importantly, a Godly Play designated space enables the children to respond to a story they have just experienced using any of the stories within the Godly Play curriculum – such as the "desert bag".[8] In my own experience, many children gravitate towards the sand and can express their own hopes and dreams very movingly. They could choose to work on another story that has just become more resonant for them, as well as today's. For a more detailed analysis, please refer to appendix 1.

If, like many of us, you cannot dedicate a room just for Godly Play, a trolley or set of shelves carefully used will suffice. The idea is that all the materials used are there and available for each child to use should they so desire. Ideally, some lessons are in woven baskets, others in gold boxes, others carefully stored along the floor. Don't forget to use as many varied forms of creative materials as you can and to vary them week-by-week. Leave the coloured pencils and felt-tip pens at home occasionally and see what the children then choose to work with.

The visual focus is of Christ in some form – perhaps a lovely hanging or tapestry. The Holy Family is there (a critical story within the Godly Play curriculum,) as is a light and the model to represent the Good Shepherd. The room is designed to give an environment that speaks to those present of God's love in Jesus.

The visual stimuli, the materials, the layout, as well as the way that the adults interact and relate to one other and the children and young people, all work on an indirect level to teach about God and the community working together. The children and young people are recognized as a community, the body of Christ, just as much as the adults who are worshipping elsewhere. There is a welcoming person, the "greeter", at the door so that everyone feels welcomed and valued as they arrive. Unlike many Sunday schools, the parents and carers leave their children at the door; it must be explained and agreed that the child/young person is entering a sacred space, where their work is play. The adults might prove distracting, and, more importantly, it is the children's space. If a child is fractious or unsettled, they stay with the greeter, to calm down and so slowly enter the special space. When the child is ready to participate, they move into a waiting circle of all the other children, with the storytelling adult already present. The storyteller greets each child/young person. They sit, forming the circle as the group arrive. They then wait for the others with quiet conversation initiated by the storyteller, as they ascertain what has been going on in each participant's life. The group is encouraged to sit with their legs crossed as a way of indicating their readiness for what is about to take place. They are opening themselves up for learning.

Development: story

Once all are ready, the storyteller will tell the story. This is very different from much storytelling today. The story is told with the help of visual aids, often wooden models. There is no eye contact between the storyteller and the children; all attention is focused on the story. The narrative words have been learned as a script; although many people struggle with this, these scripts "work" for the hearers. Many years of research, analysis, and experience have pared down the stories to the best form so there is minimal personal input from the storyteller. The aim is to provide "just the story". This method aims to draw the circle into the story, to show them how to use religious language to make meaning, and it may be that the listener also encounters God through that internalization of the language, the jargon, the special, specific vocabulary of faith, as they work through the story unfolding before their eyes. Critically, it means that every time the child/young person hears a story, the person who tells it is not important for maintaining the quality and accuracy of the story. That story remains the same, enabling the hearer to take the words and work on them over and over again, much like an adult hearing one of Jesus' parables. We have all experienced the jar of hearing a much-loved story from a new version/translation of the Bible, when the wording changes just as you arrive at the bit that you knew by heart! In my own experience, the jump from "I will make you fishers of men" to "I will make you fish for people" was quite shocking and eye widening.

The story is told slowly, the visual aids moved around the central space to reinforce the words, with plenty of pauses, so that the full power of the language can be taken in. The modern need for bigger, brasher, more exciting storytelling is not present in the Godly Play context. The aim is to give the story space to speak for itself. This can feel very strange, like putting a brake on for a child in their culture, where bigger and brasher is so much the order of the day.

My own experience of being part of a Godly Play session as a learner is that the story "sucks you in". You find stories that you've heard many times before suddenly regain their power to move and change you. It's quite extraordinary. In some way the method of storytelling seems to reclaim the imaginative power of the original teller, speaking down through the centuries in a fresh way. The other observation that I would make is that for me, the story seems to bypass my intellect and go to my emotional intelligence – the right side of the brain – in a way that few other experiences of the same story have done in the past.

Development: wondering

At the end of the story there is a time to wonder. The storyteller cues the process with some "I wonder" questions. These are designed to help the children internalize the story, to help them to be there, for example, as one of the sheep in the parable of the lost sheep. "I wonder if the sheep have names." Or, "I wonder if you've ever felt lost and heard the Good Shepherd call your name."[9] Most importantly, the "I wonder" gives permission for the children to let the story take them further, to explore the feelings and thoughts that have been aroused, either by articulating their thoughts or by staying with them internally. Their imagination has been within the story. It is a time to let their creative thinking flow, to encourage engagement with the language of the story. Critically, the storyteller does not have an end point in view. This is not about checking whether the listeners have grasped a particular concept or understood the learning outcome of the lesson. This is one of the points where Godly Play is aiming to model truly open learning. Wondering is intended to encourage children to utilize religious language for themselves and to understand such language when others use it. If any part of the process could be described as the most important part of the work of the day, it is this time of wondering, of being open and receptive.

Read the following example of a wondering session, at the end of the parable of the Good Shepherd and try to see where the children's minds and hearts have wandered. ST stands for storyteller, the responses come from a class of nine to ten-year olds in a church primary school. Note also that the storyteller gives no clues as to where she wants the conversation to go, it is driven by the children's wondering.

ST: I wonder if you've ever heard the Good Shepherd call your name? I wonder if the sheep were happy in there? I wonder where this might really be? I wonder who the sheep might really be?

Child: They could be us and the Good Shepherd could be like Jesus.

ST: Is that what you think?

Child: The sheep could be angels.

ST: The sheep could be angels?

Child: The sheep could be Jesus' followers.

Child: The sheep could be Jesus and his disciples?

ST: The sheep could be Jesus' disciples. I wonder where the sheepfold is really, and I really wonder where this (indicating the visual aid world) might really be? Now I wonder how listening to that story made you feel?

Child: Relaxed.

ST: Relaxed?

Child: Peaceful.

ST: Peaceful?

Child: Really calm.

ST: Really calm?

Child: It made me think.

ST: Made you think. What about?

Child: About... things that...

Child: It made me feel relaxed and it was good to watch because like... God like with his followers.

ST: Ah ha.

Child: ... sheep that got lost...[10]

Godly Play acknowledges that children also have fears and doubts about the meaning of life and death. The spirituality of the children and young people is being recognized, not as that of an adult "watered down" in some way, but unique and as relevant to the child or young person as that of an adult. Thus, Godly Play is taking the development of spiritual lives to be of fundamental, primary importance. It also recognizes that children and young people understand their own boundary – that there is more to life than just me and my physical presence.[11] It gives them the space to explore their relationship with the visible and the invisible world to which they are relating.

Development: responding

The group is then given a chance to respond further to the story. There is no intentional guidance as to what materials are given to direct the listener's thinking or imagination – draw, write, or create – but every child is asked to choose freely what work they would like to undertake, be it with crayons, paint, clay, Lego, or Play-Doh. Each week is not a discreet section and it may be that some want to return to a work in progress. The storyteller will ask around the circle and the greeter will assist each hearer to collect the materials they need to work on the story. The group takes time to work through creative materials to explore how the story has impacted on them. This gives the story time to register and be internalized, owned and part of their world. They are not told what to do, neither are they given materials that would control their creativity, it is the equivalent of a blank sheet and they can make of it what they will. It may be that one listener takes out one of the boxes containing stories or one of the other visual cues to a passage previously explored. This means they probably have unfinished business within that area and they are encouraged to continue that work. The responses to the storytelling can be quite startling. This is a conversation with a child, discussing the painting she produced as a response to the parable of the Good Shepherd. Note: ST stands for storyteller, L is the initial of the child.

> L: I think the story at the moment was like it was, it was probably about all the... sheep, the sheep probably felt really lonely when he was in the forest and then all his... all his other sheep came back and found him or maybe they, they got... had an argument or something and then they called him and they found that they really... that they couldn't live without him so they went back to get him.

ST: Lovely, that's lovely. Is there anything else that you want to say about the story?

L: I think that the sheep were far better when they were all back in the sheepfold and they were all together so they could just chat.

ST: Chat (laughs). So they could all chat - that's lovely.[12]

Note how the child had really entered the story – the sheep is acting in an incredibly child-like way in the listener's mind, "had an argument or something." This understanding of the story is based right in the child's world and experience, not some far-off place called "religion". And they get back together to chat! The storyteller was just as amused as you might be reading that! Here's another example:

ST: I wonder if you could tell me how the story made you feel, the story of the Good Shepherd?

J: Well, it says in the poem, it's a story of rollercoaster emotions if you will. Erm, every time the story just kept changing, all the emotions, they kept coming to me quickly.

ST: Which emotions can you remember?

J: Well, at the beginning, the beginning of the Good Shepherd, well, it's all between the beginning and the end.

ST: Uh-huh. And you've got the emotions in your poem haven't you? Can you read your poem, so that we can hear it?

J: It made me feel like I hadn't before, all that and a whole lot more. The beginning of the tale made me smile so fine my heart turned as gold as the sunshine. When the sheep drank from the water crystal-like the thought came to me like a sword strike. When the sheep got lost in a dark place gloominess spread wildly across my face. When the Good Shepherd found the lost sheep happiness returned to me as though it couldn't sleep. And that's how the poem makes me feel inside with emotions so powerful they couldn't hide.

ST: *That's a wonderful poem, J. So, today, I wonder if you could tell me how you feel about the story today, as you look back?*

J: *Well, it's quite amazing that the Good Shepherd keeps looking out for his sheep.*

ST: *Uh-huh. How does that make you feel about the Good Shepherd?*

J: *It makes me happy cos I know that he'll never, ever go out with one sheep missing.*

ST: *Who do you think the Good Shepherd is?*

J: *Jesus.*

ST: *Jesus, right. J, I think this is a really, really super piece of work. Why did you choose to write rather than do a picture?*

J: *Well because I like poems, they're my sort of thing.*

ST: *Uh-huh. That's good; you think you write better than you draw. That was really good. Thank you.*[13]

The two children mentioned above only had a single session for their entire Godly Play, but the work that it produced was quite startling in its depth and understanding, as shown by the poem.

It may be that a child will spend several sessions working on a single piece – this will not be "this week's" story but the child working on how the story touched her several sessions ago, work that needs time and energy to be completed and finished. The group works on its own, until it is time to move into the next portion of time. The materials are designed so the group can be completely responsible for getting the materials out, then cleaning up and putting them away. Work in progress is stored. "finished" work can be taken away. All work is good, for the child/young person has attended to their feelings and expressed them through the work.

Development: prayer

Once the work is put away, the children return to the circle for prayer. Again, this moves around the circle. Each may pray aloud, or silently. Their "amen" is the cue to move on. A child/young person who doesn't have a prayer may shake their head.

Development: the feast

The group then shares the feast; a drink and something to eat for each person. The group remains sitting in the circle, whilst two of them serve the feast, which is consumed together. The feast focuses on being together, not what it is being consumed, in a clear reflection of the communion that the adults may be sharing at the same time in another place. Thus, the community is built on the replaying of the over-arching story of the church, that of the Eucharist. The storyteller may talk with the children/young people about other feasts that we know of from Scripture while the food is eaten, and then they clear away, move back to the circle, and wait for their parents or carers to collect them.

Ending and leaving

As with arriving, the departure is one at a time. The storyteller will say goodbye to everyone, as will the greeter, and the children/young people leave with their families or carers.

Indirect learning

Throughout the session, the adults try to relate to one other consistently, in a respectful, supportive, and loving manner. The room is treated with respect and care; mess is cleaned up by whoever made it. "We respect each other's work" is the clear rule. The adults also recognize that the whole group sits there to learn from one other, and that listening, and giving time to the process of listening, is critical. This is the behaviour that we hope to inculcate in the children and young people, and the indirect teaching that the group experiences shows them how Christians of any age should be towards one other.

Enabling worship

The structure of the session reflects that of the Eucharist, which has come down to us through 2,000 years of worship and tradition. Within the Eucharistic structure are the cues to help people into worship, and within the environment of the Godly Play space are similar visual and aural cues designed to help the group worship. The children/young people are helped to come to the place where they can wonder, together and as individuals, and through that point of wonder, the creativity of the hearer can interact with the Spirit of God, and learning can occur and be taken into the heart. The group forms its own church, its own community, and draws from it as adults do from their own church. As with a Eucharist, the children/young people come together; they greet each other, share the story and wonder together, develop their wondering about the story through play and creativity, they pray, share food and drink, and then leave. Each moment of the time together is carefully maintained, personal, deliberate, and thoughtful. The aim is that every person feels special, appreciated, and known. The laid-back feel of each session is designed to help the individual work just as much with their interior world as they do with the external world. The measured pace of the session may feel quite weird for many who have worked in a more traditional style of Sunday school, or even one that is modelled on the education they see children and young people experiencing during the week, but I have found this slow and thoughtful method to be very helpful, especially for those who tend to be rushing through life at the pace set all too often by busy parents/carers.

Many people are reporting that children/young people with difficult, maybe dysfunctional, home lives are finding Godly Play exceptionally helpful, a real place of safety and calm amidst the mess that they live. There is almost an element of therapy at work as they are allowed to be young and taken seriously and cherished within the safety of a special place. Godly Play dedicated rooms are especially helpful here as the children/young people identify with it almost as "their church" – see appendix 1 for more analysis of this. Godly Play aims to teach all of us how to use the language of the Christian tradition to encounter God and to use that encounter to gain direction for our lives. The sessions have been devised to enable children and young people to come to God in a real and genuine manner and to take their spiritual lives seriously. In previous work,where I compared this method of storytelling with that of using puppets, it was evident that Godly Play did indeed enable the children to understand and internalize the story more effectively.[14] I would heartily endorse this method for your week-by-week teaching in Sunday school whenever that is practicable.

Questions for discussion

1. How does the thought of this type of religious education strike you?

2. What aspects of Godly Play are new to you?

3. Are there any aspects of Godly Play that you find threatening?

4. Are there any aspects of the two conversations that surprised you? If so, can you share what they were with the rest of the group?

5. What practical constraints would your church/group encounter if you were to use Godly Play regularly?

CHAPTER 9

Play

God has a book where he keeps a record of good and bad children. When we do something wrong he points a finger at us. He understands what we say even in our thoughts. He can see what we think.[1]

I want to begin this chapter by asking some very simple questions:

- What was your favourite game when you were at preschool?

- What can you remember from that time?

- What do you think that game taught you: about yourself, about others, and about how you relate to others?

From these thoughts, let's think a little more:

- How do children learn about role and gender?

- How do children learn about life and what might happen to them?

- What happens to children who don't have secure adult relationships to base those games upon?

In the family that I grew up in, and bear in mind that I was a girl and the middle child with two brothers, play was seen as something that children do and that they grow out of. Part of the story of my adult life has revolved around relearning how to play, as I'm not convinced I was that good at it as a child. I was "sensible" and "very grown up" from the day I was born, and it was only once I became an adolescent and joined a drama group that I began to play seriously. Maybe this is one of the reasons that I so love Godly Play, as I see "sensible" children being given permission to do what they need to do within their childlikeness, within safe boundaries, and I wish that I had experienced that as a child too.

Keith J. White in his book *The Growth of Love* speaks of a child's need for:

- Security

- Boundaries

- Significance

- Community

- Creativity[2]

White wrote this book after many years of fostering children, many of whom were on their "last chance" within the system, who were so damaged and hurt by their life experience up to the point of coming to live with White and his family. This gives him unusual insight into how children and young people are damaged by poor parenting as they grow up, and his experience of ministering in such a context gives us the ability to hear his wisdom. Looking at the above list of a child's deep needs, we need to explore how each word impacts upon the development, learning, and identity formation of an individual (for instance, what happens if they're either not there or not adhered to?). Because a "good" parent will be running on an internal script that includes all of the above, and assuming you are such a person, you may be surprised to see the list in black and white, thinking, "Well, isn't it obvious?" But to a parent who hasn't had such an upbringing, the answer to that question is that it's only obvious that small people, and not so small as well, have those aspects included in their life if they are fairly secure in themselves, and many parents tragically are not. And, like the need to play, that need never goes away.

The Good Childhood Report (published by the Children's Society in 2009) says that in order to flourish children need:

- Loving families

- Friends

- Positive lifestyle
- Values
- Good schools
- Mental health
- Enough money[3]

This report, never cheerful reading, explores how these different aspects of life are required for children and young people to be healthy and happy – a different take on White's list, but implying the same needs.[4] In a hugely moving scene in *Les Misérables* by Victor Hugo, when Jean Valjean at last finds the young Cosette, he gives her a doll, Catherine. She takes it under the table and immediately starts to play with it. Until now she has been the slave of the family, treated worse than a dog, yet at last she is shown love, and she responds by playing.

Without these aspects of life, children will be insecure, unhappy, and their subsequent inability to relate in a healthy manner means they will not have the space to be able to be whole human beings, as expressed through their play.

Let's explore more deeply what White is saying in *The Growth of Love*. His home and extended family attempts to create an environment that will do justice to the tension between the "here and now" and the "not yet" of childhood.[5] Childhood can be seen as "before adulthood", yet we need to allow children to explore who they are as they grow up within this creative tension – it's like Christians who live in the "not yet" of the kingdom of God; we wait, living as if it's just around the corner. We have to make the most of the moment that we live in. Life is not about living for the time in so many years when we might feel as if we have arrived as an adult – for when does that happen? As surely that we live as if the kingdom of God is coming, eventually, so let's live as well as we can now. White values the creative tension between the two interwoven modes of existence – on the one hand, play, daydreaming, and messing about, mainly located in the present, on the other, education and nurture, which tend to look ahead.

It is in the playground and the playtimes, the nooks and crannies, the dreams, and the spaces between lessons and sessions that some of the most important growth of self-esteem, community and creativity emerges.[6] A school recently banned children from speaking as they moved from one lesson to the next. How sad, and truly ignorant, is that? Children need to let off steam, and deal with what is important to them at that point in time, not balancing chemical equations, much as I would have loved that when I was teaching. It is in the break times and the lunchtimes that children can be themselves in safety. What did you play when you were at school? I remember being chased by a boy called Michael, who was the dalek. I was about eight at the time. My children played "raptor attack" all over the house for about six months in 1993-4 – *Jurassic Park* strikes again![7] Through these games we establish boundaries and much more, as well as running off energy. At secondary level young people establish identity and peer groups in between lessons, as they share their lives and become themselves. We need to provide safe spaces for this development to be facilitated.

Where do we say the most significant things? They rarely come up when we have set up a careful environment with a candle and Bible. Far more likely as you play a game together, work in a garden, or do a jigsaw (all types of play.) Side-by-side conversations are often the deepest. And side-by-side playing can open up deep conversations; just don't play expecting profound conversions.

Which brings us to a tricky question: what about boundaries? Boundaries are at the most fundamental level of our being – truly instinctive. They give us our personal security, and without security there is no growth. If you don't feel safe, then you don't play, and you don't trust. Maslow's hierarchy of needs tells us that once we have the physical requirements for living, such as a roof over our heads, a peaceful environment, enough to eat and drink, then security is the second most necessary requirement for life.[8] There is no space for exploration, wistfulness, spontaneous experiments, conversation, games, dances, or play without security and boundaries. If the world is unpredictable and unreliable, there is little scope for the experimentation that development requires. How do you play if you don't know what's really going on in your life? Or do the games begin to reflect the life you find yourself in, with guns, knives, and drugs in the worst examples? How do young men and women see the adults in their lives treating each other, and how will that have been played at when they were younger? A psychiatrist can often spot a psychopath as a child by the games that they play.

One of the overriding questions for us as adults working with children and young people is quite basic: how do I maintain good boundaries? For example, who are you friends with on Facebook or who do you follow on Twitter, not to mention all the other types of social media sites? If you are in paid ministry are you effectively living "over the shop", and available 24/7? Is that right? How do your family feel about that? You need to lay down rules about how accessible you are and let your family and group know those rules and then keep them. That may need strategies and carful planning, but it will be worth it.

Personal significance, a belief that *I'm worth it, God loves me for who I am,* embraces self-esteem and identity, and emerges from a secure and predictable context, with a sense of belonging to a wider community than just me and my immediate family. I need friends who are not family, as well as family who are friends.

If community has to be wider than the nuclear family – and for many children (and their carers/parents) the best example of community will be their local church or school – we need to ask ourselves: what sort of community is the focus of my work? If it is just the church-based community, then how is that community maintained outside of the group functions/meetings/events? How does this community play together in a safe way? Do the children and young people I work with realize that I am part of this wider community too? Do they see me engaging with the wider community of the church and the school? Does the church engage with the school in a meaningful way? If not, why not, and what can you do to open up this enlarging of the community?

Creativity is part of the development process but may also be a bi-product. All children are born creative and given the right conditions (as defined by *The Good Childhood Report*, and also by White) will flourish.[9] Adults who say "I'm not a creative person" have had their creativity knocked out of them by life, but given the right conditions, it will return. I speak from personal experience. Creativity is essential for language development, without which everything else starts to stall, another important gift of the Godly Play experience. One of the basic aims of Godly Play is to equip the children with a religious vocabulary. That sounds like a very grandiose aim, but when do we acquire the very specific jargon that the Christian faith runs on? How do we know what "redemption" or "sin", or "grace" mean? Godly Play allows children to explore such enormous concepts and arrive at a meaningful understanding of such words and be able to use them.

Interestingly, creativity is now part of Ofsted's inspection criteria for "Spirituality". We are most like God when we are being creative, and children are at peak creativity when they are playing. It doesn't feature highly in many of our religious liturgies, the creative part is often in the creation of the piece, so it is worth considering how we enable adults to be creative and to play within worship. The music or the flower arrangements are highly creative, but I don't know many flower arrangers who would thank me for describing this very clever form of art as play. And while musicians "play" music, it's usually rather a serious piece of playing.

Language starts with movement, gestures, and inflections – described as the "dance between mother and child."[10] We see parents talking endlessly to their children, often about nothing important, but what is going on is the sharing of language. A recent BBC2 series *Babies: Their Wonderful World* (2018) explored the importance of language in babies and toddlers up to two years, and parents were found to average about ten thousand words a day with their child. The link was clearly drawn between acquiring a rich vocabulary and how successful a child is at school, and we all know that children who are bathed in language are the ones who speak most fluently. Always remember that some children could have a disability that impairs speech, and that Word style children will remember words more effectively than the other three styles. There is concern amongst educators that many children do not engage in conversation with adults enough, not just because the caregiver is using a phone, but because we often live separate lives, in our separate spaces once a family is at home – together but apart.

Humour and jokes may be the highest level of communication. When people can laugh together, then there is real community and shared understanding.[11] Humour requires lots of thinking to understand and is often highly located in culture. It requires the ability to throw ideas around in your head to make the wrong connections, but connections that will make people smile and laugh; a very high order of thinking. I love the books of Terry Pratchett for his ability to use language in a way that pulls the rug from under my feet and makes me laugh out loud – so clever and so unusual. We know that laughter sets hormones running through our bodies and is so good for our wellbeing. Laughing as we play has to be how we learn the language of God, reflecting the joy of creation and of love. Children often use humour in their games, often "toilet humour" which will reduce them to hopeless laughter. And they may well repeat their joke endlessly. It's a stage, go with it.

So we come to that critical question – that of the role of story. Why do people so love stories? What's your favourite story? Are they essential for mental wellbeing? Eugene Peterson says, "Story is the most natural way of enlarging and deepening our sense of reality, and then enlisting us as participants in it. Stories open doors to areas or aspects of life that we didn't know were there… or supposed were out of bounds to us… Stories are verbal acts of hospitality."[12]

Watch children playing in a school playground and see the endless variations of play. As I said earlier, my own children at about seven or eight years would shout out "raptor attack!," scream, and run furiously. I remember playing *Doctor Who* with my friend

Michael, who was always a dalek and chased me. Both these games are based upon stories we saw on a screen, but equally valid, In both games the children are playing at being chased by a monster, a major theme of Grimm's fairy tales, and very important in learning how to be afraid and how to process such strong emotions. At the time of writing, *Peppa Pig* is flavour of the month for many preschoolers, and they will set up tea parties and other scenarios for their own "Peppa" and her family and friends. Horror stories and films go on being popular – we need to be frightened so that we can at least have some idea of how to cope should that thing really happen to us. And children also need to practice strong emotions, to manage them when they are really happening, through bereavement or other life circumstance.

Each person is born with the innate ability to learn and share through stories.[13] What's happening to us when we listen to a story? We will each hear a slightly different story as we place ourselves within the narrative through our imaginations. Thus, we can "practise" difficult events before they arise, we can gain empathy, see another's point of view, and be educated as to how other people live, or lived. Years ago, the BBC produced a radio programme called *Something to Think About* for Key Stage 1 assemblies. It always included a story, and at the end of the year the listeners were asked to nominate their favourite story, to hear again. What did they ask for? *Badger's Parting Gift*.[14] It's the story of how badger dies, and his friends in their grief come to realize that badger left them each a gift through their friendships. It also includes a beautiful section describing how badger experiences his death and passage to an afterlife. *Badger's Parting Gift* deals with death – something most parents shy away from with their own children. It enables children to see how death may not be all bad, and gives a more reflective feel to such an event.

Whenever we hear a story, we have our own unique version of the tale in our heads. Something that is ours, and ours alone. We hear something that relates to us differently from how it relates to others. Godly Play recognizes this and asks the listeners, "I wonder where you are in this story?" and each listener is invited to appreciate that where they are might be completely different from anyone else, and that's OK. Sometimes we adults need to remember this. White says in *The Growth of Love*, "No one will ever know how each child's imaginary setting and characters differ from those of the next."[15]

Think of how different every single "home" is. Now expand that to consider how very different every child or young person's life is – and their own story too. We cannot go there, we can only go part of the way.

White goes on to say, "Without stories and storytelling, a child's imagination is deprived of the stimulus to create and shape images and pictures into coherent pictures and narratives."[16] A child needs this exercise of the imagination, not least to arrive at some sense of their own life story. How else can they develop a sense of identity and continuity with the mass of sensations that they have experienced and make up their biography?[17]

The way human beings engage with story is complex and sophisticated. Why else would we pay money to watch a film, TV, or read a book? These things are critical to our wellbeing in a subtle and rarely appreciated way. Stories are employed by therapists as they help children to deal with trauma, and to work out how their lives have been hurt, with the possibility of healing and wholeness through giving the story another ending. Story is the essence of play. No wonder Jesus told stories – we never grow out of them. Novels continue to be written, and the popularity of audio books tells us how much we enjoy listening to a story as well as reading one. And, as someone who is hooked on audiobooks, it is a very different experience.

Never underestimate the place of story in our culture, as it may well not be coming in the form of a book. It has been estimated that before a child enters school they will have been exposed to 30,000 advertisements in the course of their short lives. Advertising is where our children receive their basic grasp of the world's meaning.[18] If you want to be convinced, take the time to watch episode seven of the final series of the TV programme *Mad Men*, where the gathered advertising executives talk about the place of story within the advertising world. We need to ask ourselves as ministers: how does this impact our work? Look around the environment that your children and young people occupy – what are they being told every day through various images, through their phones? How do they see themselves within the story that the environment holds? How does that affect the way they play?

The power of creation is the power of articulation and without a new articulation there is no new seeing, so every creative act is a new act of articulation. "Creation is the process: articulation is the product."[19]

Through our play, our "making up" of stories, we articulate who we are and we find our place in the world. Possibly the most important story is that of who I am, within my family, and those stories are infinitely varied. Never assume anything about the stories that our children and young people carry within them; they are not the same as your own.

So, we come back to this little word that we have been unpacking now for quite a while: what is play? Maria Montessori (1870-1952) said that play is the child's work, and the theory of education that bears her name is witness to this aphorism. Godly Play is very much based in her theory, allowing the children to be self-led and seeing each person as innately spiritual.

Play is re-creation. The enormous range and depth of such re-creation, however, is too often overlooked. Many see playing as a superficial or trivial act, but I see it as a life-giving act.[20]

Do we recognize the work of God going on within our children and young people as we "allow" them to play? Do we honour the healing process at work as children and young people play, or do we channel their activity within our church groups towards producing something that tells other adults that we have indeed been teaching the children

*about God? That we have been preaching "the gospel" in
our session, rather than letting the gospel take root within
the children and young people? Is that teaching about
God preventing the work of God within that child? Hard,
challenging questions, but we need to engage with what
we are doing carefully, for we have precious work. In my
own years in ministry, I discovered that the sermons that
were most appreciated and commented upon were the ones
where I retold one of our Bible readings for the day; not
with a moral at the end, just a story to take with ourselves
at the end of the worship and to mull over.*[21]

We need to think about where God is in our play, and I recommend
another writer, John Pridmore, and his amazing perception about
where and how children play.

*It is at this boundary between land and sea, between here
where we are safe, and there where, most certainly, we are
not safe, children play. Children play on the shore, close
to the water's edge. We grown-ups move far "inland", as
Wordsworth puts it. We retreat to our deckchairs and
newspapers higher up the beach, if not back to our desks
and laptops.*[22]

Last summer I sat on a beach and watched this going on; children
(who I don't think knew each other as friends) came together and
were very busy at the water's edge. They gathered water and sand in
buckets and seriously took it higher up the beach to build a castle.
There was some organization by the older children, but they were
running to and fro and along the edge of the water with smiles and
laughter. They were being children and having the time of their
lives.

I have already mentioned the work of Rabbi Sandy Sasso. In
her beautiful book *God In Between* she tells the story of how an
elderly couple recognize that we find God in the space between

us.[23] Winnicott, a psychologist working many years ago, speaks of the "third space" – the physical space between you and me as we interact, to which we bring our own meaning. He is cited in Berryman: "Playing takes place in the intermediate and overlapping area of experience between the 'me' and the 'not me.'"[24] This area is a place of spontaneity, it is a space where we each bring a contribution, and where those contributions meld and mix to give us far more than the sum of the parts, where play can become far more than "just play." Berryman continues, "The significant moment in such experiencing is when the child or adult at play surprises himself or herself with a glimpse of the true self."[25]

Often in Godly Play, we hear a child say or do something which is astounding and we wonder how that came about. It comes because we provided a safe space (see chapter 8 and appendix 1 for more) for the child to truly explore the story and listen to the meaning that it brings.

If we can only wait, (the patient) arrives at understanding creatively and with immense joy, and I now enjoy this joy more than I used to enjoy the sense of having been clever. The principle is that it is the patient, and only the patient who has the answers.[26]

It is so hard to do what Winnicott is talking about here; we don't tell what the story means, we wait for the story to speak to each listener, and so we unleash the innate creativity of those who hear and the power of the story itself. We find God in the "in between" us.

Rebecca Nye believes that good play is satisfying, done largely for its own sake (a process rather than a product) and it can draw us into uncharted waters (imagination, deeper relationships) and can't be forced, and therefore it is suggestive of things at the heart of Christian spiritual life. Could we say that play has certain sacred qualities, which in turn are at the heart of a child's life?[27] Nye says,

*This recommends that we should particularly look out for
the sacred in play and be more alert to playfulness in the
sacred.*[28]

Play is a universal feature of human societies. We find it across the
globe, and similarly undertaken by children, especially when away
from adults. White says:

*Constructs' of childhoods have changed over time... but
it is the nature of a child to want to play in one way or
another.*[29] *I believe that is perhaps the best and most subtle
constituent element in the emotional, social, physical and
spiritual growth of children... It is not that we need to
organise sport and play for children and young people,
but that we should continue to create and preserve spaces,
physical and emotional, in which they can play and use
their imaginations.*[30]

Most play for children operates in the non-logical, non-verbal
realms of language – it is just a "being" activity, perhaps a form of
what we might call "mindfulness", totally in the moment, totally
spontaneous. But the real difficulty is in the translation process, in
the interpretation from one language to another. When we watch
children, how do we know what on earth they are really doing,
re-enacting? It's the problem of being "lost in translation". Adults
prefer to operate in the logical world, the world of words and
ideas. Children come later to this, when some of their remarkable
spontaneity and creativity has been "honed". As Pridmore says,
that is far safer, but in that safety we risk sanitizing God.

Original visions can vanish, in the telling, in the "adult-eration".
We adults like to interpret, to dig down and ask questions that
are sometimes intrusive and for our own benefit. Privett further
comments that play *is* the "opposite of emptiness"[31] and that for
playing children there is a "relationship with 'flow' – a state of
joy, creativity and total involvement, in which problems disappear

and there is an exhilarating feeling of transcendence."[32]

We are back to the God in between. The creative, spontaneous God who is there in the middle of the children's play, which we in our culture often undervalue and cut short. We need to let the children and young people play, and so find God playing with them.

Questions for discussion

1. How do you play?
2. How does God play?

CHAPTER 10

Children thinking about God

When I think about God I think about chickens.
Oscar, four years old

Throughout this book there are various comments from children about their spirituality and day-to-day experiences in the world. Most of them relate directly to God or to church, which ties down the breadth of spirituality that is present in children but gives an idea of how diverse the thinking of children can be.

This chapter will look at some of the comments that I collected, trying to unpack what might lie behind each comment.[1] I have arranged them in order of content and age, so we start with the youngest, hopefully seeing a more "developed" image of God as the children's ages increase. It may be beneficial to remind yourself about Fowler and Westerhoff's theories of faith development, as well as the chapter about cognitive development, before reading on and seeing if you can relate to what the children are saying, and their approach to God, with what these two theories propose.

When I think about God I think about my little sister.

George, four year old

George is a nursery/reception-aged child who has made a direct relationship between the God who creates and gives life, and his little sister, about whom we know nothing. I'm assuming that George loves his sister, and that his feeling towards her and God is that of thankfulness and love. This comment (and most of the others) was logged just before Christmas, with the Christmas nativity play happening daily in rehearsals, so it could be that George is thinking Christmas, a baby, and so to his sister. It's a comment that shows an appreciation of the wonder of creation, love, and family.

When I think about God I think about chickens.

Oscar, four years old

This is simpler than it might seem at first! Oscar's family keep chickens, so I read here that Oscar thinks of home when he thinks about God. The word "home" is a massive concept, which increases in complexity as you get older. For Oscar though, home is a good place to be, with chickens. So thinking about God gives Oscar chickens on the mind. The other possible thread here is that chickens lay eggs, which are used for food, once again, positive images of life and sustenance for a four-year-old. There may even be a tie-in back to Easter and the images of eggs and new life.

I think about how lucky I am to have a loving family.

Jordan, eleven years old

This gratitude for a loving home persists in Jordan, at the top end of the school. God means loving family, with all the ramifications about security and bonding, and Jordan is now aware enough to know that not everyone has one of these – so he thanks God for this great base to work from. Jordan is equating God with love, love that is both given and received.

I think about God when my grandpa died and I was sad.

Tamas, six years old

I think about God when I am all alone. I think about when I am dead.

Tamara, six years old

I remember that he is making the world a very happy place. I remember when my mum told me about my great-grandfather who fought in the war and how he is still alive now.

Emily, eight years old

I think about my grandad. His name was Sidney. I did not get to see him, he died.

Sydney, eight years old

We tend not to talk to children about death. We want to shield them from the pain and difficulty that adults inevitably have in dealing with death, so we pretend that children don't need to know about it. We also don't want to talk about death ourselves. This is a defining point about our present society; we choose not to encourage children to go there either. In fact, children have interesting thoughts about death that can bring joy in the midst of grief – like the comment elsewhere of a child seeing her deceased grandfather in the sun. They also have a lot of work to do in their own growing up that is concerned with recognizing death and their own mortality. They are aware that talking about death is hard for adults, and it's been my experience that once children know that my work includes dealing with death and bereavement, the questions come tumbling out. These are basic questions that children need to consider and ponder at their own speed. We need to be careful here about giving children the idea that adults don't talk about death any more than they talk about spirituality.[2] Our desire to protect our children from the tougher side of life is possibly doing more harm than we realize in the long term.

Christianity is predicated on the death of Jesus, and children entering churches will be met with crosses and depictions of the crucifixion. If our faith is based on the death and resurrection of God's Son, we must be prepared to help the children as they deal with the extraordinarily challenging and complex idea of salvation and atonement. Christians are rarely honest about the knotty questions within this concept and area of belief; at theological college we studied ten different models of atonement, from the early church up to fairly recently, and I had problems relating to all of them! My favourite model is expounded in the classic, *Can These Dry Bones Live?* by Frances Young.[3] The conundrum of a loving God sending his Son to die is difficult enough for adults, let alone children. I firmly believe that we don't know, and probably couldn't get our heads around, what took place through that death and resurrection other than that our relationship with God was changed for all time in a truly mysterious and incomprehensible way. My personal belief is that to teach a more simplistic, formulaic version of salvation is possibly not going to help anyone, but to actively help children struggle and work towards a great mystery is a better thing to do. It's allowing the Spirit of God to work within the child's imagination, and that's a risky business, but I firmly believe that the Spirit of God is better working with a child's faith than my words! If you find that challenging, then so do I.

One of the things children find difficult, as do we all, is picturing what a soul is like. When my own four-year-old wanted to know where his (deceased) granny was and what had happened to her body, I tried to explain something along the lines that she didn't need her body anymore, so only the bit that made her granny was still alive, and that was with God in heaven. My son replied, "So she's like a ball, bouncing around?"

A helpful image that a friend gave me when I repeated this story is to talk of the dead person leaving their body behind rather like taking off a layer of clothes.[4]

Children appreciate that living things die, and that something of that person (or, as far as a child is concerned, pet) continues with God. Hence the relating of God and death that we see from Tamas. Children realize quite young that their parents will die too, leaving them in the world. This is a huge issue for children to come to terms with, and best handled with care, but always letting the child talk when they need to about this difficult area.

In my collection of children's thinking, death frequently occurs. Children need to be taken seriously when they ask about death, not fobbed off. Tamara is quite clearly aware of her mortality, and is musing on it, but her thinking about death is difficult for me to contemplate – I might try to change her subject onto something a little more cheerful. But why should I assume that Tamara is being morbid? The problem is within us and our culture, which likes to avoid thinking about our own mortality. That such a discussion reminds the adult of their own mortality (which may have very different connotations from a child's mortality) is undoubtedly why we try to turn the conversation.

Emily is older and finds the idea of eternal life a great comfort when trying to deal with the problem of her forbears being dead, yet part of her parents' memories. She may also have realized the comfort that this gives to her mother. Sydney is clearly pleased to share his grandad's name, despite never having met the older Sidney. Again, thinking about God helps when pondering death and our mortality, as the clear belief here is that Sydney Jr will eventually meet Sidney Sr.

This ability to be with difficult thoughts which pertain to the spiritual is indicative of the children's own vast resources in the area of spirituality, and their intuitive understanding is in startling contrast to most adults'.

> *I think about God when I am alone in the dark and I am*
> *scared without anyone with me.*
>
> **Abigail, six years old**

Abigail is scared of the dark. So am I if I'm honest, and our hearts go out to her as she speaks of her fear. It's a natural instinct to be scared of the dark. When we lived in tribes and possibly caves, you were more likely to be eaten in the night than in the day as our eyes don't work so well then, and the night is the resting time for humans, but not for all predators. The other aspect of being scared now is our natural creativity. If I wasn't busy imagining what might be under the bed, or creeping up the stairs, I wouldn't be so frightened.

But Abigail thinks about God at this time; the one person who is there in the dark with her when she's alone. God is acting here as a parent or friend, someone to be there for her at a time when she would otherwise be lonely. Night-time is traditionally associated with God dealing with people. It was in the time when they were alone that God spoke to many of the prophets in the Bible, and later to Mary and to Zachariah. People interviewed in more recent days acknowledge more spiritual experiences when they are alone. Being alone in the dark opens our minds, as we can't see images to control our thoughts. Our creativity is given expression through our imaginative thoughts, and then again, our deepest selves can speak to us through our dreams. It's a good and natural thing to think about God when we're alone in the dark.

> *When I think of God, it makes me happy and I say prayers*
> *to him, and he listens to me all the time! Thank you, God!*

Joshua, seven years old

Joshua's comment is charmingly worded but is concerned with Joshua and what God does for him, and contrasts with Kamran's comment below. But Joshua is typical of a child of this age, and it's worth looking at what he has to say. Piaget points out to us that children of this age are egocentric; parents can never give them all the time that the child would take if given open access; so God can be there 100 per cent for Joshua. God listens to Joshua all the time. Joshua has understood that God is there for him always, and his faith is shining through. Joshua says his prayers, which are, I assume, very much of the "God bless Mummy and Daddy" type but are important for him. Certainly, the prayers at assembly/ collective worship with children of this age are by necessity quite simple, although they don't need to be simplistic.[5] Children of this age will often write prayers that tend towards one-liners, but usually profound and to the point. Joshua's comment is also worth noting because God makes him happy. This is a very up-beat contribution. How many adult Christians act as if, or say, God makes them happy?

> *I think that he is strong and lovely and cares for all of us.*

Kamran, seven years old

In Kamran's comment we see several aspects of a child's understanding of God's personality. Firstly, God is male, both in the "he" and the "strong", which could be used about a woman, but probably wouldn't be, and then we also have God is lovely; lovely person or lovely to look at? Does it matter? It's an unusual adjective to use about God, and usually ascribed to a woman when used to describe physicality. And finally, God cares for us. Put the whole thing together and the gender of God is far more blurred: lovely, strong and caring.

Kamran's comment is imaginative and very affectionate in its tone. In terms of his concept of God, Kamran is moving towards his own internalized understanding well; this is not as egocentric as many comments from children of this age. If we contrast with Joshua's comment above, you see the breadth of spiritual understanding in children of this age. This may be affected by the household that the two boys come from (but which I do not know – the following comment arises from hunch, not knowledge); I hope that a strongly religious family would, through ongoing conversations and practice, enable children to work on their concept of God in a way that would not be so accessible to a child from a more secular background.

A helpful, caring man.

Charlie, eight years old

I think of an old man in the clouds.

Joseph, eight years old

I think of God sitting high on his throne watching down on us.

Isobel, nine years old

Charlie, Joseph, and Isobel articulate the classic child's view of God. Where does this view come from? We don't have the beard, but we have the old man on the throne. Many children go through this stage, reflecting a distance between us and God, and will also say that heaven is "up there". Perhaps it comes from images of God seen in pictures – the Sistine Chapel, Blake's *Elohim Creating Adam*, or perhaps the most powerful people that they know are kings and queens, who tend to be imagined as older, on thrones. Helpful and caring give us the classic, grandfather concept of God. Notice that these children don't seem to have heard about the God who sits in judgment, although a distant God could be read in these comments, a God who is watching rather than acting.

I wonder what he does and what he looks like.

Ciaran, eight years old

Ciaran's comment appeals to me enormously – a child wondering in an open and honest way about what God is really like and what he does. Ciaran has appreciated God is not like us and doesn't "work" as we do, so what does he do? How does God do his work? And what is he really like? This is an open and very attractive spirituality. The problem for me is that I would like to suggest the answers to Ciaran, and why should I presume to know the answers? These are questions that the wise will leave to the young to answer. The way to help Ciaran move on might be to ask carefully worded questions of the "I wonder" variety, to help Ciaran think through his thoughts about the activity of God in the world, and whether God "looks like" anything that we might recognize at all.

I see Jesus and him in my mind in heaven together.

Henry, eight years old

Henry has moved onto purely Christian thinking about God. Jesus is seemingly a more straightforward concept than God, so to think about Jesus with God marks Henry's thinking as more specifically Christian than the thoughts we have encountered so far. The fact of Jesus is very important within the Christian faith, as Jesus gives

God an (imagined) face, and the historical reality of personhood, like people we see in our day-to-day lives. For members of other faiths, this insight into the person of God must be quite enviable. For those who are forbidden to make any sort of representation of God, Jesus must seem like a real bonus! The big negative of Jesus is that he underlines the male gender of God that we keep seeing in these children's comments and that most of them will hold onto as they grow older.

I love God, and that he will be looking after my brother in heaven.

Ellie, eight years old

This comment brings us back to the story of St Freddie in chapter 2. It is still a horrible fact of life that some people die young and some babies don't get to grow up. Ellie's brother, and Freddie, are two such early deaths that left sisters trying to come to terms with the baby brother who died. Having a belief in God who looks after the dead is surely of great value to these children. When they get older they may then ask the unanswerable "why", but as yet they haven't got to that stage. People who can ask "why" and get no answer, yet still hold onto their faith, have entered Fowler's stage 4 and may well have travelled through it to stage 5, usually being many years older than Ellie.

A friend who had a miscarriage suffered from recurring depression for years after the event. Eventually, she asked God to show her the lost child, and she had a dream, but in the dream the baby was now the right age – he was about seven. So she accepted that, eventually, she would meet the child that died so young, and that his life hadn't actually ended with his earthly death, he was growing up in heaven.

For many Christians, this belief that we will meet our loved ones again after our own death is very important. When dealing with our own bereavements, such a belief can be a real anchor in the storm of grief. Children seem to have no problem with the concept of continuity, including the idea that life could "begin" before we are born; in our heavenly existence that prefigures earthly life.

There is nothing wrong or bad about God.

Callum B, eight years old

This is a classic comment from a child, in that no adult would say this. Read it again and appreciate the purity of the child-like faith. Callum clearly has an understanding of what is wrong or bad, and he defines God by saying God is not that.[6] He could have said God is good and right – an adult might choose to use longer words to say that – but Callum defines God by excluding the qualities that he recognizes as sinful (although I wonder if he even knows that word?). There is a real sense of awe, and of understanding the truth about what is in the heart of God in this simple statement. It is to such as these that the kingdom of heaven belongs.

When I think about God I be [sic] silent.

Callum C, eight years old

This comment comes from another Callum, but once again resonates with insight. As above, Callum C is developing a sense of God that is awesome, that is beginning to delve into the abstract, the infinite nature of God. It is usually a mature adult Christian who says that when they think of God, they come to silence. This child modestly writes his few words that might sum up years of pilgrimage.

When I think of God I picture angels gliding around a light in a dark and starry place.

Emelye, eight years old

I see a king on a throne, but he doesn't have a throne or a cloak, he is just dressed the same as the other people.

Ryan, nine years old

I imagine what he looks like and think if he is a lady or a man or even a thing (but not an animal).

Gregor, nine yeas old

I think that he is not in the sky, he is in the world.

Mitchell, nine years old

I think of massive light and clouds and everyone living life to the extreme.

Sam, nine years old

Can you hear the thinking processes going on in this selection? These are children who are all about the same age, and we clearly see that some of them have lost the image of God in the sky, whilst others are still there. The angels in the dark and starry place is the simple view of heaven as up in the sky. The king on the throne but dressed as other people shows that the idea of God's kingship being different is fomenting in Ryan's mind. If God isn't a king like a regular king, then what is God like? Children of this age often describe people by their exterior, so we have the comment about cloaks and crowns. Gregor is still puzzled by the bodily appearance of God – everyone else he knows is either male or female, and while God can be a thing, God can't be an animal. It's worth staying with Gregor – this is a really honest comment, clearly showing his concepts being ratcheted into the next stage of Piagetian cognitive theory. Gregor understands that God cannot be categorized in the way that everything else that he has come across can. And this is the only comment that I received from this cohort of children that God could be either male or female, but God's probably neither.

Ryan and Gregor are both in the process of moving from the king on the throne towards what we see in Mitchell's comment – he's not in the sky, he is in the world. Mitchell's God is omnipresent, and again, unique to this cohort of children.

Sam's comments about living life to the extreme (perhaps a

paraphrase of John 10:10, "I came that they might have life, and have it abundantly," or perhaps a reflection of too many "extreme sport" video games) are unusual. Sam sees life with God as more; "more extreme" is hard to comprehend without talking further with Sam, but he clearly sees that the life of faith has advantages over that of no faith. Light is always a positive image, and Sam sees the light as God. Interestingly, there are also clouds, perhaps to hide behind, or perhaps to make the picture of a sunny, summer sky. Perhaps the clouds reflect Sam's learning that life has good and bad patches, but that God is with Sam no matter what.[7]

> *I think that if God didn't exist then we would not exist either, so I think of that every time someone mentions God.*
>
> **Andrew, nine years old**

> *I say to myself, "I wouldn't be here if God didn't make the world."*
>
> **Oliver, nine years old**

> *I ask myself all sorts of questions about God. What is he like? Will I ever see him? Will I go to heaven or hell?*
>
> **Shaquille, ten years old**

> *I think he is like the key to the world and without him the world wouldn't be a good place to live.*
>
> **Caroline, nine years old**

This group of children fix their ideas of God in that of the almighty creator, the omnipotent God. These are the beginnings of real philosophical thought beginning to take root, as these children chew the cud internally over the question of the nature of God. They are clearly well into the third stage of Piagetian thought, with concrete operations evident in the way that they are thinking and expressing themselves. The children are still clearly committed to God being there, and not seeming to doubt God's existence yet, although the questions are the precursors to some of the big philosophical/religious questions that we all confront: Does God exist? What is the nature of God really like? How can we find out?

Some of the children have begun to enter this later, more questioning stage:

> *I think of God always looking over the world, and he's the happiness inside us.*
>
> **Kirsty, eleven years old**

> *He sits in a golden circle, which is heaven looking at the whole earth.*
>
> **Alexander, ten years old**

> *I think that God and I are in a garden chatting to each other about flowers in the garden.*
>
> **Megan, ten years old**

> *I think about God as a huge hand coming with blinding light and gives me comfort when I die where I'll go.*
>
> **Chris, ten years old**

> *I think of a face in the clouds, watching everyone and everything.*
>
> **Emma, eleven years old**

> *I think of a bright spiritual light shining amongst entire darkness.*
>
> **Alex, eleven years old**

> *I find him like the godfather of the world. A great big powerful man.*
>
> **Tom, eleven years old**

In this selection of comments from children in the same age group at school, the big differences are clearly showing between them. The comments vary from a quite sophisticated idea, of the golden circle around the globe, to the godfather image, which I find rather scary! From the face in the clouds, through the godfather, to the huge hand with blinding light, these children are tussling with God internally, working on a definition for the indefinable. The awe that we have seen so much previously is still evident, and the nature of God is shifting even more towards the omnipotent. I wonder if these children would still give me such open views in a year's time, when they've begun at a secondary school, their hormones have started to rage, and peer pressure to conform to the secular norm is becoming stronger.

I become calm!

Brandon, eleven years old

My hopes and pleas seem to come true and my worries go away.

James, eleven years old

I see myself with him.

Jack, nine years old

These short, simple statements are very pleasing to read. These reflect for me a healthy faith in these children. Calm feelings, prayers coming true, worries receding, seeing oneself with God, these children are talking of a real relationship with God in an honest and affecting manner. These are children who have learned about faith and have now internalized and own their faith.

I think about whether he is real or not and if he is what does he look like.

Eleanor, nine years old

Eleanor is displaying the classic existential thought – does God exist? Some would say that the fact that Eleanor is wondering whether God exists tells us that actually God must do, as we clearly spend a lot of time wondering about this thing we call God.[8] Yet she still wonders what God looks like. Is this a feature of the society that we live in, where appearances are so important, and, as previously mentioned, especially important to children? We need to ask Eleanor again in a few years, when she has come to an answer as to whether God exists, if it matters what he looks like. For now, she is still thinking about a God who has some sort of bodily attributes. Eleanor's wondering is healthy and good; the fact she is wondering shows us that her spiritual life is alive and well.

I don't believe in God.

Louie, ten years old

I don't believe in God, because he would have stopped all war.

Mikiel, ten years old

I don't really believe in him because I think, how was God made, how did God come to be?

Ellis, ten years old

Well, I don't think about God. In assembly I don't say the prayer.

Arun, ten years old

If God is almighty why doesn't he answer our prayers or help?

Alex, ten years old

So we arrive at a group of children who have decided to give up childish ways. Of the entire cohort, only one other response like this was present, from a four-year-old, who replied, "I don't know". Maybe it's cheating, but I read that as "I don't know about God," rather than "I don't believe in God." This group have decided, for reasons that we hear all around us, that God doesn't exist at all. Ellis's wondering about who made God is a classic in a child, often younger than Ellis, and not something that adults often say.

I'm pleased these children felt able to be truthful in this way, and that they have now arrived at a faith that excludes God. Bearing in mind the school they attend is strongly Christian, it's great that these children have come to a real questioning of God and felt able to reflect that to me. (Remember, you don't have to believe in God to have faith or a personal spirituality that is alive and well.) Giving children permission to say what they really think, rather than what they think I want them to say, is critical, but hard to achieve in the present school system. How do I know the other children were being honest and not just writing down what they thought they wanted me to hear them say? This wanting to please, and give "the right answer", as well as going along with the rest of the group, was bound to skew some of the comments that the children have made. My concern is always whether these really are the children's thought-through decisions, or if they are merely copying the words that they hear around them at school and at home.

However, there were a few comments that I would like to finish with that need a little more unpacking, as they refer back to work that I have previously entered into with the children, some quite a long time ago.

I think of sheep and purple velvet robes.

Victoria, eleven years old

Every year, I work with the year six children in RE when they are studying the "I am" statements of Jesus. I go in and tell them the story of the "good shepherd"[9] (John 10 mixed with Psalm 23), using Godly Play as the method. This was many months ago, and it has clearly fixed in Victoria's mind. She does not say in what context she thinks of sheep, and who the sheep stand for, but this is a comment about the value of Godly Play as a teaching method – Victoria clearly internalized the parable when she heard it told a good while ago.

The purple velvet robes? This must be a reflection on Easter and the story of Good Friday, which is eight months before she wrote her thoughts down. The purple robes paired with the sheep represent an unusual combination.

Both of these comments, about the sheep and the robes, illustrate the way children hold things in their mind, often for far longer than an adult would. When I was in school researching for some writing, I used the "good shepherd" Godly Play. One child drew a picture of the disciples, including Judas hanging himself. This seemed at first to have little relationship to the good shepherd, or the season, which was just before Christmas. This boy had been thinking, albeit probably at a subconscious level, about Judas hanging himself for eight months. My work that day gave him the opportunity to open up and work on that disturbing story once more. As adults, we find this challenging, but as people who work regularly with children, we should always be open and alert to children referring to stories and events that we have dusted down and stored away many weeks previously.

> *Jesus is the saviour of the world. A candle burns with holy fire, when the candle is blown out the fire is gone, Jesus is gone, but he will return again.*

Charlotte, nine years old

On Ascension Day, I took a candle into school and based my assembly story around the Godly Play story of Ascension – a difficult concept for adults, let alone children.[10] Charlotte's comments tell the story pretty much as I did: a lit candle stands for Jesus, the light of the world. The candle was extinguished using an egg cup "snuffer" and we watched the smoke curl upward and outwards and then smelt the air. The explanation is that the flame hasn't gone, it's just changed as it goes out. Charlotte has fed the story back to me, seven months after she heard it. I think that's pretty remarkable! Be encouraged when stories don't seem to be instantly "successful". This assembly was regarded by the staff as one of my more unusual ones, and they seemed fairly perplexed at the end, yet Charlotte held onto it, and that way of telling the story has fed Charlotte, once again, for many months.

I hope these comments are useful to you. Taking time to unpack the seemingly simple comments of children is a worthwhile exercise and helps us to see God through their eyes. It draws us nearer to understanding children understanding God.

Questions for discussion

1. Share some of the comments that your children have made with one other and see if you can take the children's comments and reflect on them together. What is God saying to you through these children?

2. How do you handle children who want to talk about death?

3. What seems to be the predominant "hang-up" with the children that you work with? How do you stay with the children in their concern, helping them to work on the issue?

4. What can you remember of your Sunday school teaching? What does this tell you about the best way to approach your own children?

CHAPTER 11

Home, school, and church: how do we work together for the benefit of the child?

God has little stars in his hair because He lives among the stars… from there He tickles everyone's head, but we can't see it.[1]

Every year Canterbury Diocese invites church primary schools to a Cathedral Schools Day. These events have been running for years and I find them absolutely wonderful. Around 300 children attend, with teachers and other willing volunteers, all to explore Canterbury Cathedral through workshops, prayer stations, and worship. The noise when they arrive is astounding! But at the end of the day, the children lead us in worship, including writing and leading us in the prayers, and others do the talk. The clerical person who is there to introduce and close the worship (a member of the cathedral chapter, the Bishop or the Archdeacon) is duly amazed by the calibre of what the children say and do. One year I heard a child pray that the "Archbishop and Bishop would feel God's arms around them." Never before or since have I been so moved whist praying for the Archbishop and Bishop. Afterwards, I heard one cleric ask the children who had given a first-rate talk which church they attend. They didn't. And if they did, would they be leading the worship in this way? I like to think they they that would, but have yet to experience such a thing, unless it was a special "one-off" service. A city church in Canterbury has such a service, once a term, where children and young people lead all the worship, apart from the few sections that (in the Anglican church) a priest must lead. Being a very middle-towards-high Anglican church, it uses the liturgy and has Communion every week, so the children and young people who take over have to give way to a priest for part of the service. It was the responsibility of the curate to, dare I say, curate the service. She had come across the idea at Greenbelt festival and had suitably aged children herself. The time I attended, the "tinies" led the prayers, using Duplo bricks and with the adults steering them hard. The nine to ten-year-olds led the service, very well, and a duet of teens did the talk. It was very well structured, audible, and produced the "rent a crowd" type congregation of family members all glowing with pride. Many were from a local estate, where the church has a daughter church, and would not have found their way to this church except for special events. At the end, all those who had led the service were in the procession out, and the "regulars" were clearly thrilled by what had taken place, delighted to have so many younger people worshipping with them that day. All in all, a great success, and the home-made cupcakes which we were fed afterwards completed a very successful act of worship. But it's only once a term, and the curate is now vicar in a different place. I don't know if she's started these services there. I have a feeling she needs to find the children and young people to lead first. Ironically for someone who works for the diocesan education team, when I spoke to the older children who had preached, it turned out that they attended a local Catholic school, not the Anglican secondary.

One of the biggest motivations behind the Cathedral Schools Days is to let the children know that Canterbury is their cathedral. For some parishes and schools, Canterbury is a long way away (many will have travelled for around an hour to be with us), and they may not think of going to the cathedral anyway. Perhaps more prescient for us, however, is how do we enable children and their families to regard the local church as *their* church, and know that if they were to attend, they would be welcomed and worship would be appropriate and accessible? How can we encourage churches, schools, and families to work together for the benefit of a spiritually active child?

Let's start with the church. Every school in England (sorry if you're not reading this in England, but it's all I know) has a parish church, and most parish churches have at least one school, sometimes five or six. They may be "church" schools, or what I am going to refer to as "community" schools, although church schools often have both roles. This means that the incumbent (vicar/rector/whatever you call the person in charge) has a potential congregation of little and not so little people in one building that is not the church, and I would strongly recommend getting in there! Not to openly evangelize, but simply to be there, to be known, and to offer support in any way they can. Most schools badly need such a friend but won't welcome someone who goes in with conversions in mind.

My own experience with community schools tells me that heads, and especially secondary heads, if you can befriend them, desperately need a safe place to dump some of the awful things that they deal with, secure in the knowledge that it will stay within the four walls. You could volunteer to be a governor, always in short supply, you could offer to lead collective worship, or to help with trips such as Cathedral Schools Days. There is a multitude of ways to be in the building and be known as safe.

I was school chaplain at a large comprehensive school in my second parish, and found myself taking assemblies, which took six working mornings every half term – one day per year group and one for the sixth form. I even took them when Ofsted were in, for which the head was eternally grateful! It was seemingly costly time-wise, but all the students knew me. As I also took funerals for parents, grandparents, and even a teacher, this knowledge and trust of me was invaluable.

A further tip for ministers who are involved in local schools: If you have a dog, try and walk it at going home time at least once a week, and then you'll find yourself getting to know parents and carers as the children and young people talk to the dog.[2] (Obviously, the dog has to be OK with this.) Being known at the local school makes you part of the community and has many helpful aspects, one of which is that the families will know who you are if and when they arrive at church. Now that may be only at Christmas (and the children will be far more enthusiastic to come to church if they know you, and think you know them), but slowly you will get to be trusted. These families may never become Sunday regulars, but that's not what I'm talking about here. I'm talking about enabling families to grow as spiritual people. Your church will be their church, a sense of ownership and belonging even if your congregation doesn't agree with the terms of engagement.

If your local school is a "church" school, then the children and young people will possibly have a better knowledge of Christianity than their parents/carers. Over recent years, the extra inspection criteria (currently referred to as "SIAMS": the Statutory Inspection of Anglican and Methodist Schools) has tightened up in an extraordinary way. Church schools' acts of collective worship will include language taken from the Anglican liturgy such as "The Lord is here; His spirit is with us" at the beginning of worship, and a blessing or grace at the end. A Bible story will be included, and children will reflect upon life as Christians, all in the subtle "but we don't assume you're Christians" way that is a fine art form.[3] Church schools normally expect their local incumbent to be involved, or to have a team of people who do it instead, for not all incumbents are "good with children", and if yours isn't, but thinks they are, then you're going to need to have a polite chat with them.

If the local incumbent is involved in the school, then drawing links between home, church, and school should be easier. They can get involved in planning the worship. Church schools now encourage their students to be involved in planning, leading, and evaluating worship, so they could get involved in that group as well. They can befriend the head, or whoever has responsibility for worship, and give support there. They could offer to be the governor with oversight for RE and/or worship, always remembering the law about such matters.[4]

Encourage your incumbent to go on a course on how to lead collective worship – the local Anglican diocese will probably run them, and if they don't, do ask. Most Anglican ministers do not get trained in this aspect, so will be going on memories of when they were at school, and we probably don't want that. Recent research indicates that the willingness of the local church to be involved in the local schools, however costly time wise, pays back massively in terms of facilitating the spirituality of the children.[5] Fowler tells us that these children may well seem to lose their interest in spirituality as they go through secondary school, but Westerhoff tells us that if, as with the children/young people leading worship, children and young people are *valued* members of a local church community, they have a far higher chance of remaining in that worshipping community as they go through those troubled teenaged years. If your incumbent isn't gifted in this way, what can you do? Take a look at appendix 1 at the end of this book. It outlines how two people ran super Godly Play-based clubs after school.

Here's another story of how one person got involved in her children's schools with fantastic consequences. A local church vicar spotted great potential in one of the Sunday school parents – let's call her Jo. Jo has been part of the local church all her life, and is married with two young boys, one has just started at the local church primary school. The vicar was going on a three-day Godly Play training course and talked Jo into going with her.[6] The fact that Jo has no idea what Godly Play is didn't stop this plan from going ahead and both came back full of ideas and enthusiasm about using Godly Play at the local school. The vicar talked to the head and they arrived at a two-pronged approach: Firstly, over the course of a half term, about six to eight weeks, every child would visit the church, over the road, in a half-class group. Jo would tell them this term's Godly Play story there, aided and assisted by members of the congregation. The children would hear the story, engage in the wondering questions together, and then go back to school for their creative response time. Jo also told the story to the mid-week Communion congregation, and while they engaged with the wondering questions, they didn't use the creative response time during the worship, although they could when they get home. This proved immensely popular. Secondly, Jo started a Godly Play after-school club, once a fortnight (as this gives her time to learn and resource a new story), for up to sixteen children. Jo also now uses Godly Play stories at the Messy Church that she runs whenever that is appropriate.

I can only say "bingo!" in response to this story. The children love going to church for the story – it's almost like a trip as they cross the road and enter the church. They now view the church as "their" church. They meet local people who worship there and know them by name. Perhaps more importantly, the children are known by members of the congregation, who can welcome them when they arrive on a Sunday, or at Messy Church. The children engage with Godly Play, which widens their experience of Bible stories and enables them to engage with language that they might otherwise have missed out on, as well as pondering the nature of Christianity and their place within or without it.

The after-school club is fascinating. It is oversubscribed, and many of the children who attend are what might be described as "troubled" children, children who have baggage from home, which they can unpack and explore within the safety of a Godly Play session. It has become their safe space.

The period from Ascension Day to Pentecost is used by my diocese for a "novena of prayer". It has become more widely known as a result of the "Thy Kingdom Come"[7] initiative, for which I have been part of the team providing resources. Jo used the intergenerational resources provided to set up prayer stations in the school for the period, which proved very popular with the children. And she was asked by some parents to provide resources for them too – parents who do not attend church – which she duly did. Jo has become known as the unofficial "God person" within the school, with parents asking for her prayers and counsel at the school gate, and she has opened up the church for many who would not have seen themselves as church-type people a few years ago. She has now undergone some lay ministry (not ordained) training, and is wondering where God is leading her in her life whist ministering in this fantastic way at a local school, on behalf of the local church.

There is a perceived problem for many young parents, in that many are not confident, of how to facilitate their own spirituality as well as that of their children. This is very much a Western problem. On a recent trip to Japan, I watched a queue of people praying at a temple, queuing up to address the gods. I was thrilled to see a girl of about nine queuing with her younger brother and their parents. When it was their turn, she carefully showed her brother what to do – to clap hands and then place them together as you respectfully bow and pause.[8] Her family had taught her how to pray, and she was now teaching her younger brother. Children who go to our church schools may find themselves teaching younger children how to pray, as indeed they do through leading worship. But many of our middle generation, the thirty plus group that are so under-represented in many churches, simply don't have the experience or the knowledge of how to pray, or recognize when they are in touch with their own spirituality. How do we discreetly enable such families to move on together? As part of my work with Canterbury, I have devised what we call "prayer packs" in collaboration with a local ministry couple, Steven and Lesley Hardy. We did the first one as a response to a local vicar, in a tough part of Canterbury, who asked us to give his congregation ideas of how they could pray. This congregation does everything they can as intergenerationally as they can (see chapter 12) so the prayer pack was designed for parents/carers to use with children together[9]

Here's an example.

Using sand to pray

Put some sand into a large, clean, litter tray. Make sure that it's "play sand" rather than builder's sand.

Let your fingers run through the sand. How does that make you feel? Now smooth the surface, as if God is smoothing your heart. Now write in the sand, either something that is hurting you, or something you are sorry about, and then rub it out as you are forgiven, or you forgive.

Prayer stations have become more popular of late, encouraging people who are not strongly Word style, or of a more active learning style, to pray in ways that they might find more helpful. If you want ideas for active prayer, look at www.prayerstationsinschools.com for more ideas than you could possibly want! You may want to personalize them for your particular context, but they are all prayer activities that families can do together, and so grow together.

Here's another simple example:

Marble prayer activity

You will need a bag of marbles and some foil, cut into small squares that are big enough to wrap a marble in, and a container for the discarded foil.

Choose a marble from the bag, and look at it for a while. How beautiful is it? What colours can you see? How was the colour put inside? Now wrap the foil around it. This is how sin – the times we muck up and do things wrong or upset people – can cover the person we really are, and God wants us to be, underneath.

Hold the marble and think of the wrong things you have done this week. Ask God to forgive you and take away the foil as a sign that your sins have been removed. Now look at the beauty revealed.

There are more ideas for families who want to grow together in chapter 12.

* * *

How do we enable schools and families to work together more effectively for the child?

This is an easier area than the church-home link, as all schools contact parents/carers on a regular basis, and with some forethought schools could easily send weekly ideas home in the newsletter, as many Roman Catholic schools do already.

A good place to start might be during one of the more important religious festivals, such as Advent or Lent. If the school were to follow the Advent prayer pack scheme, then it would be easy to take one of the activities and send it home to parents/carers to use with their children. As one of the earliest activities is a recipe for

Christmas pudding, and how to pray as you make it, you would need to send the link home before Advent starts, and possibly organize the school to buy in some of the ingredients, perhaps selling "pudding packs" to families who want to have a go. Many families don't stock baking items such as currants, and as you only need a relatively small quantity, it makes sense for the school to be involved here. It might be that children make a pudding at an after-school club, which parents pay for when they pick them up. It's better value than a shop-bought pudding, and as it's the recipe that I use every year I can vouch for it being delicious and quite forgiving for inexperienced cooks.

Another way to enable children and adult to flourish together might be to use a resource such as the "Easter experience".[10] This super experience needs the church and school to collaborate, using adults as guides for children and their families as they walk through the Easter story. Families are invited to come to the church to do this together in Holy Week, or another convenient time, and many conversations ensue. Again, relationships between school families and people who worship at the church are opened up, making the transition into regular church easier.

Other schools use prayer stations in schools and set up a room with a variety of prayer stations, which students visit during the day and families can visit after school, always with amazing results. Both churches and families have one talent which we rarely think of sharing with the local school – that of gardening. Many schools have a gardening club and areas of school ground that could be cared for by such a club. Teachers have lots of things to do after school, but why not volunteer to help the children to learn how to care for their immediate environment? Safeguarding provision will have to be carefully followed, but older people are often keen gardeners and would be happy to share that talent with the local school. And as many older people now have grandchildren living at a distance, they can come alongside children and become very special people in their lives. It would be a regular commitment, but it would pay vast dividends, especially for men, who are often uncomfortable working inside a school building with children, but could prove amazing role models for children, especially boys, who may not have enough men in their lives through no fault of their own.

Many schools open up their collective worship on a regular basis for parents to come along, and some of these ideas could also be shared through that arena. But it needs a carefully thought through strategy, and lots of support from the local church.

Finally, if you have a church school in your area, have you ever thought of inviting the head to come and address your congregation, either through a short sermon, or at your church meeting? A regular commitment to pray for each other would be enormously beneficial.

- Could the school choir take part in your carol service?

- Could you help out with the school's nativity play, perhaps by making costumes?

- Could your skilled sewing people offer to make banners to enhance the worship in the school?

- Could you work with the children to make banners for the worship area, or reception?

- Could you buy the school a Godly Play set, such as "The Holy Family" for display in reception at Christmas time?

There are so many ways in which churches, schools, and homes can work together, but in our busy lives we rarely manage to achieve this joined-up thinking. Perhaps, having read this chapter, you could begin to share ideas with others, and open up the lines of communication that will be appreciated by so many.

Questions for discussion

1. How could your church offer to help your local schools in the ways we've been thinking about?

2. How do you support your minister in their relationship with the local schools?

3. How regularly does your church pray for local schools, and the heads, by name?

Chapter 12

The way forward: growing faith

Ayesha looked up at the stars shining in the night star.
"Hello Grandad," she said.
Ayesha, five years old

It is clear to those of us who are committed to ministering with children and young people that we may need to rethink a lot of the work that we do in churches and associated groups. Are we respecting children and young people in their spirituality? Do we allow them to participate in their group fully? By this I mean to be part of the planning and evaluation of the sessions, so that they can really do the things that are helpful and lead to spiritual flourishing, rather than repeating the stuff that I liked doing when I was their age? In my last parish the children of the choir asked if they could have a junior PCC, to meet and talk about the agenda for forthcoming PCCs so that they could contribute.[1] And this was a very encouraging and successful idea. The children frequently have far more imaginative and inclusive ideas than the adults do. I have already talked about the Cathedral Schools Days, where the children lead the worship and the talks, and in church schools pupils are now expected to regularly evaluate the worship and suggest ways to improve it. For some of us, this is a real shock! By sharing the running of our groups, we say so much to the children and young people, following Westerhoff's suggestion that they need to be profoundly involved in the faith group if they are to move forward in their faith formation and be part of "the way we do things here". It is what happens in our church and community schools, and it needs to become what happens in our churches and associated groups.

I believe how we approach nurturing faith comes down to some basic questions that question our attitude profoundly.

Is our role to minister *to* children or *with* them?

If you look at advertisements from churches looking for people to fill posts such as youth workers or family ministers, all too often the expression within the text is "to minister to young people" or "to minister to our young families." Underlying that stance is the idea that in our ministry we are doing *to* people of whatever age, not joining *with* them in a mutual ministry. Is our life of faith a journey, side by side, or one where we stand ahead, giving instructions as to how to arrive at the point that we occupy today? I sometimes think ministers can feel like those people with ear defenders and fluorescent paddles at airports, waving the planes onto their stands!

Can children be fellow pilgrims or do we hold the knowledge?

"Fellow pilgrims" is an expression coined by my boss at Canterbury, Murray Wilkinson, to describe a mutuality in the way that we minister – I hope to be blessed by you, you hope to be blessed by me. We are eye to eye as we travel together despite an age difference. We all know that children bless us through their immediate spirituality – enabling us to share the moment of ordinary grace – but do we recognize how profound that mutual sharing can be? And if we recognize children and young people as fellow pilgrims, we come to the next question.

Are we teaching facts or nurturing faith? Are we enabling the two to go on side by side?[2]

For many group leaders, the responsibility of teaching the faith, of handing on the story, weigh heavy with us. In reality, much of our teaching is about God, not being with God. As the home page of the UK Godly Play website says: "In most religious education children are told who God is. In Godly Play children discover who God is."[3] This is a subtle but massive difference, and the falling numbers of children and young people in church indicate that what we've been doing hasn't worked too well, so maybe it's time to re-think? Obviously, Godly Play is making a huge claim for itself, and if you can't manage Godly Play on a regular basis then we need to look at what else is out there for ideas. There is a quite delightful Pixar short film called *La Luna*, which is a parable for us all and can be watched again and again, each time with the viewer seeing something different and noteworthy.[4] It tells the story of three generations of men who sail out together into the sea. They go up to the moon and, by a process of sweeping up, make the full moon into a new moon. You need to watch it to understand it, but the clearest message coming from the film is that all three generations learn from each other, and it is by listening to one other and learning from one other that they work out how to do the job in hand. The young boy is every bit as important as his father or grandfather, and each generation engages with the work in hand in a different way. I cannot recommend the film highly enough, and it's only about seven minutes long.

The argument for intergenerational working is made without language. Without listening and learning from each other, the task in hand would have failed. Intergenerational worship – where everyone is there all the time all the way through – is not the same as "all age". Intergenerational worship is where everybody is worshipping together. Not a service that has been adapted through having a "talk for children", or even activities for children. This is about everyone coming to worship and recognizing that there needs to be give and take on all sides and everyone needs to be heard. It involves mutuality, equality, and reciprocity, and aims to become the culture rather than a curriculum or programme. In worship, it may involve a change in seating – many churches run a "café style" church, where everyone eats as well as worships. Round tables are ideal, but the whole service needs to be carefully planned to include everyone. Most adults don't recognize that when they speak the children and young people will go quiet, so we have to listen and include younger voices carefully before the adults do the usual "taking over".

Westerhoff tells us that for children to be included effectively we need to share the following:

- **Story**. Both the story of who we are – how did this worshipping congregation come together, how did we change over the years, what is the story of each family – as well as the story of salvation.[5]

- **Authority**. Who has the authority in this group and how is it given? Many churches have people who assume authority despite never being "given" it by those who are officially in charge. Facing that coup and sorting out who is really in charge is painful, and something that many churches avoid noticing, let alone dealing with.[6]

- **Ritual**. What do we do together that marks our life as a community? How do we mark birthdays, festivals? How do we welcome new members in? How do we say goodbye to those who leave, either through moving away or death? How do we deal with people leaving because they don't want to be with us anymore?

- **Life**. How do we share our day-to-day lives? Do we know what work others do, what the children and young people are doing at school, college, or university? Do we even know which school, college, or university they are part of? How do we support those who are finding life difficult at the moment? How do we share success?

By including children and young people in all of the above, we become more intergenerational, as the unspoken message is that we value what the children and young people bring and want their input in the day-to-day experience of our lives, partly so that we can pray in an informed way, but mainly because we care and value them. Importantly, intergenerational worship can be introduced slowly – perhaps just for a couple of festivals to begin with, along with a change in how you work to make the community more intergenerational – but this is a massive shift for many, indeed most churches and worshipping communities, so we're looking at change over years, not days.

An example of this is All Saints in Canterbury.[7] This church is in quite a tough area of a relatively wealthy city, and the Sunday worship is often as the whole church family together. One of the ways of sharing responsibilities for the worship is what is referred to as "the rota that isn't a rota". For this, the names of various parts of the liturgy (Church of England Communion) – for example, read the gospel, lead the intercessions – are on laminated sheets of paper left at the back of the church. All the "kit" for Communion – the cup and plate (paten and chalice), bread and wine, and pieces of cloth required are also at the back of the church, along with the collection plates. As people and families arrive, they pick up one of the pieces of paper and then take responsibility for that part of the liturgy. It may be as straightforward as lighting the candles, or handing out the hymn books, or as complicated as leading the prayers, but they know that that is their part of the service and they will do it to the best of their ability. The only section of the service that isn't on the rota is those parts that have to be done by a priest, such as the words of consecration in the Communion prayer and the blessing at the end. As the present vicar, Phil Grieg, says, "It can be chaotic, but it can also be great." Most importantly, adults can find themselves being ministered to by children, and they won't think that is unusual; here, it is normal. Phil himself says this:

When I first arrived at All Saints Communion was celebrated once a month at our 11 a.m. service, and at this service we have about forty adults and twenty-eight children. The children and young people would leave just before the confession and stay out until the Eucharistic prayer was said. Then they would file in for Communion, receive it, and to my astonishment, they would file out back into the hall again. I didn't feel that this reflected "communion" in any way, shape, or form. There was little demonstration or understanding that Communion was a whole community event, and even though children were receiving bread and wine, it was clear there was no sense of awe and wonder about what this sacrament was supposed to be.

I had a church youth worker at the time and I discussed with her that this needed to change and change quickly. I was unhappy that the children and young people were sent off into groups for such a long time, and that they went out again, no sense of community or even worshipping with families, or as a family.

During my theological training I had the opportunity to visit the House for All Sinners and Saints in Denver, Colorado. I had always had a hate-hate relationship with liturgy, particularly Communion worship liturgy, but it wasn't until I visited this Lutheran church that my eyes were opened to what you could do with liturgy, and it was frustratingly and yet beautifully simple. At this church individuals were invited to take a part of the liturgy and lead it from their seat. The opening sentences, the prayer of preparation, call to confession, the peace, and so on; this was more than just someone doing the reading or leading prayers, people were involved all through the liturgy. For me, it was the first time I saw a genuine example of liturgy being "the work of the people". The priest who led the service took responsibility for the absolution, sermon, and Eucharist.

When I sat down with my youth worker to think about how to make our Communion service "a work of the people" I remembered the House for All Sinners and Saints and I wondered if we could do something similar. How wonderful would it be for a church community (of all ages) to be involved leading liturgy? We chose Eucharistic prayer D – "This is his story. This is our song". The way this Eucharistic prayer is divided tells the story of Easter beautifully, so we take the candles off the table, and with

*the corporal (one of the cloths), the chalice and paten, and
a cross we place all the items into a treasure chest. I read
out the introductory paragraph of the Eucharistic prayer,
inviting everyone to the Lord's table, and then I ask for the
candles – a child, young person, or adult comes forward
and brings the candles to me then reads out the story of
Jesus coming to be the Light of the world. We do the same
for the corporal, the chalice and paten, and the cross. The
whole congregation join in with the refrain, "This is his/our
story". I then finish with the consecration prayer and we
share Communion, all ages, together.*

*Having different voices tell the story of our faith keeps
it alive for us; there are young and old voices, different
generations keeping the faith alive in the way they retell the
story.*

Could your church try this, even once? I wonder what the worst
thing that could happen is?

For a fascinating account (originally a report to the church
council) of an intergenerational 'Messy Christmas' type event, run
midweek in a town church, see appendix 2.

Mary Hawes, who is National Children and Youth Adviser
for the Church of England, leads such a service in a very different
social context, that of Teddington in West London, and she has
devised the following acronym for intergenerational worship:

- **W**onder. Children are noted for their "awe and wonder" moments.
  In *La Luna* it is a child who stares open mouthed at the rising
  moon, so enabling his father and grandfather to recapture their
  awe and wonder at the moon and her beauty. These are often
  MOGs (Moments of Ordinary Grace), but the trick for adults is
  to recognize that what we may now take for granted may have
  been a moment of awe and wonder for us once upon a time.

- **O**penness. Have we come to worship expecting to be touched by
  God's Spirit, and are we open to whoever might be bringing that

blessing to us? Or do we have set expectations of what the service will "do for me", thus removing the awe and wonder moment, the fleeting joy of something understood or recognized, either once again, or for the first time?

- **R**elationship. Worship only works through relationship, as we see modelled in the Trinity. Who we become friends with seems fairly haphazard to me. Across ages and generations, there are some people that we recognize as kindred spirits, and so through worshipping intergenerationally we make ourselves available to everyone who is gathered for friendship. A recent Channel 4 series, *Old People's Home for 4 Year Olds*, showed this clearly. When a nursery class became part of the day-to-day lives of a group of older people at a retirement village, the children gravitated towards people seemingly at random and became very fond of "their" person or people. As the relationships were unpacked, so we discovered that many had similar backgrounds or life experiences, and somehow the children intuited this and it became a great bond. Children and young people make friends with adults who like them, often who are like them, and they sense it.

- **S**pace. As in spiritual styles, space is both literal and metaphorical. Children or young people confined in a small space will become fidgety, put out their limbs to claim more room, and annoy each other. As do adults. Give everyone enough room, but also include silence, time to breathe and internalize, time for the Spirit to move and inspire. Don't rush, despite the difficulty many adults have with silence.

- **H**ospitality. Often this comes down to two questions – what sort of biscuits do you serve, and is there someone who stops children having more than one? And for the adults – is there decent coffee, and is there a saint in your community who ensures no one is outside of the coffee cliques? We might say we're friendly, but practice often gives that an unintentional lie. No church wants to be unfriendly, but ask any visiting minister and they'll have a story of drinking coffee and watching the regulars chat.[8] And if there are biscuit police, it will impact on the children very quickly. Let their parents do that and you can engage them in a conversation.

- **Imagination.** All religious belief involves imagination as we can't prove God exists. And if you engage the imagination of all worshippers, then they are set free. Children don't have a problem with creativity, it sort of gets knocked out of us by the education system in this country, and most of the Western world, so encouraging everyone to be imaginative together is empowering and brings us closer to the creator God.

- **Participation.** The question is not "what can the children or young people do?" but "what can't they do?" Do we save the "better" jobs for the adults? When I introduced the choir children to reading the Bible passages as normal in the main service in my last parish, I had a complaint from one of the adults, as he so loved doing that and now he didn't do it as often. People don't show the same enthusiasm for cleaning up after a service. When I introduced young people as part of the rota for servers (helping the minister with laying out the Communion) some adults were concerned that they "wouldn't do it properly." They probably didn't do it in the same way as some of the adults, but who decides what "properly" is? It seems to me that we each minister as we minister, and that means variation along the way.

Notice what the acronym spells?

Importantly, at this church in Teddington all jobs can be equally shared out, and after a while that will be the norm.

All worship needs a basic structure, and I suggest the following:

- **Gather.** We come together. It's always a good idea to begin with a greeting, ideally responsive – "The Lord is here/ His Spirit is with us" type of thing – and then a song or hymn that you sing together. Singing gives people time for their minds to catch up with their bodies and to really "arrive" in the worship space.

- **Listen**. The Bible is read. One reading if this is an informal service with lots of people who aren't familiar with church, or two if your congregation has been coming for a while and they are becoming more comfortable with listening to the Bible being read and unpacked as part of the worship. Don't include a reading just because you think you ought to.

- **Respond**. In formal worship, this might be a sermon or talk. In intergenerational worship it's more inclusive to discuss and have some creative materials for the response time, as in Godly Play. You might set out a few "I wonder" questions, or just have a leader who knows how to include even the quietest (but with Symbol spiritual style sensitivity) person in the discussion. If you have creative materials, always include Play-Doh. Adults love it and can "doodle" with their hands with it while talking. It gives them a chance to be creative, while not forcing them to share what they have made, and many adults, especially activist learners, like to do something with their hands to stop them from fidgeting. I find Play-Doh does this perfectly. The prayers are also part of this section, but you need to separate the talk and the prayers by something active to keep most people's attention.

- **Celebrate**. Worship sometimes seems to forget that it's supposed to be a celebration, so what is there to celebrate, alongside God's love in Jesus? Birthdays? Medals from school or the Olympic games? A wedding anniversary or the arrival of a new baby? Most weeks there will be something to celebrate, so do make sure that you do. How you celebrate depends on the community, but cake always goes down well with me.

- **Send**. At the end of every act of worship, we need to send out the gathered community, reminding them that what has just gone on wasn't in isolation from the rest of their lives. Go and celebrate

God's love with your friends and neighbours, work colleagues, and those who you struggle to love! We mustn't stay here in isolation from the rest of the world, our mission is to be God's love for that world.

Intergenerational worship aims at *being* church, not just coming to church, and when we achieve that, then faith will grow and we become fellow pilgrims together.

Alongside Mary's WORSHIP, there is another acronym that I feel is very important, and this comes from Rebecca Nye.[9] She uses SPIRIT to sum up the conditions she believes are necessary to facilitate spirituality, and although Nye is using it with regards to children's spirituality, it is equally true for adults, and thus for intergenerational worship.

- **S**pace. As per Mary's model, with every possible understanding of the word. Adults are so bad at waiting, in quiet. If we are to internalize the worship we are taking part in, we have to slow down and give time. We also need to think about the physical environment. If you haven't read the chapter on Spiritual styles (chapter 4), do that now – the physical environment has a huge impact on our lives and our spirituality. If you want proof, try sending the adults out to the children's room one week, and keep the children in the worship area of the church!

- **P**rocess. Spirituality is a process, not a product. You cannot measure it, and it is only when you take the time to reflect as a group as well as an individual that you can see that we have moved together along the journey of faith. You cannot rush it, you just have to be attentive and wait.

- **I**magination. Once again, free the imagination of everyone present. Listen to ideas from anyone and encourage creative thinking. Try the "I wonder" style of questioning that is Godly Play's forte and see what happens when there are no right and wrong answers.

- **R**elationship. As per the WORSHIP model, we need to be in relationship with each other if we are truly to be the body of Christ. This requires more than the occasional Sunday commitment, and takes time.

- **I**ntimacy. A tricky word in these safeguarding days! But children will only share profound thoughts with someone who they both know and trust, and the same is true of adults. If we are genuinely fellow pilgrims, sharing our lives together will go deeper, but never, ever, put someone in the position where you expect them to share any aspect of their life with a relative stranger without their prior agreement and strict confidentiality rules being agreed. And, even then, let them be silent if they want to be silent, it is their right.[10]

- **T**rust. We need to be able to trust fellow pilgrims with our lives and dependability. This means being honest and knowing when you need to involve another person. If a safeguarding issue arises, tell the person that you need to tell someone else about it – and this is not optional, it is the law. A word about safeguarding: You must have a nominated safeguarding officer for your worshipping group. This person needs to be involved if you have any disquiet about the life and conditions of any children, young people, or vulnerable adults in your community. They will know if the situation needs to be escalated up in the institution that you belong to.

Many people will be thinking Messy Church fulfills these requirements, and when done well, "Messy" may indeed be intergenerational worship. But it's all too easy for "Messy" to become a type of toddler group, where the adults don't engage but sit and talk while their children are occupied. Intergenerational Messy is a wonderful thing but it may not be what you have happening in your Messy Church.[11] I personally think it's easier to use Godly Play within an intergenerational context than to lead good Messy Church, but it's a matter of taste and tradition. If you want to use Godly Play within intergenerational worship, could I suggest a few ground rules?

- If you want to tell the story with the whole congregation at the same time, think carefully about how you do it. I have told the story on a large table, set in the centre of the space. Children stand immediately in front of the table, in the round, with larger children and then young people and adults standing behind.

- Don't let the adults take part in the wondering aloud while you tell the story. If they do, then the children especially will stop contributing. As this is a great opportunity for the adults in the room to benefit from the wisdom of children, keep the adults silent!

- Send the group back to mixed-aged tables to share the wondering questions together. This will need skilled facilitators (each with a copy of the questions) who understand how this works – you're going to have to demonstrate as part of their training before the session.

- Keep the creative response materials separate, so everyone can come and pick up what they want themselves. Don't let the adults organize the children and young people.

- Give the creative response plenty of time.

Remember that in Godly Play we don't share our learning unless we want to, so do be careful how you continue together after the Godly Play input. Finally, do take note about the time plan here; this is a process which takes years, so begin slowly and hopefully any who might not appreciate what you are trying to do won't be leaving the church quickly! And good luck. Those of us who work in this field are mostly convinced that this is the new way of being church, and nothing of worth is easy to give birth to. Even in the church.

Questions for discussion

1. Who in your worshipping community holds the power?

2. Who could you talk to about introducing intergenerational worship, and what training would you like?

3. How can you enable the whole worshipping community to go forward together as an intergenerational community?

CHAPTER 13

A sharing of good practice

I'm not part of the body, cos I don't get any bread.
> **James, four years old**, at Communion, in response to
> the bidding "We break this bread to share in the body
> of Christ / Though we are many, we are all one body
> because we all share one bread."

Officially, the Church of England has, for many years, made it possible for children to take Communion before they are confirmed. Every diocese has a method where churches apply to the bishop, run a course, and then the children receive Communion. Criteria for admission vary enormously, but the basic premise is that the child is baptized and their parents support them. Many dioceses specify from age seven upwards, presumably drawing on the ancient Jesuit idea that it is at seven that you become accountable. Others allow children at any age to receive. (The Orthodox Church gives Communion at the point of baptism and onwards.)

It's difficult to say how revolutionary this is for some older members of the church, who "had to wait until they were confirmed" but it indicates that we are slowly recognizing children as fellow pilgrims, and their spirituality as a given. The quote above was my son, and he convinced me that he clearly understood exactly what was going on during Communion: he was being left out. As he was a child without a volume control, I still wonder what the rest of the congregation thought about this erudite comment.

This chapter is offered as a pattern about how to proceed with a possibly difficult issue, outlining how to manage both adults and children in the process, but more importantly giving an example of a "mixed media" course for children, with the possibility of running it as an intergenerational course. In the spring of 2006, my (then) church took the decision to admit children to Communion prior to their being confirmed. This chapter outlines the process by which the church arrived at that decision, and then the course that I devised with my curate to lead the children up to the great day itself.[1] Should your church decide to go down this path, please contact your diocesan children's officer, or equivalent, for guidance as to how you should proceed.[2]

Issues around children receiving Communion prior to confirmation include the following:

- At baptism, we believe children become full members of the Christian church. Surely that should include receiving Communion, as in the Orthodox Church?

- Children perceive not receiving Communion as excluding them, not taking them seriously. Offering this to them gives concrete action to our words of acceptance.

- If children receive Communion, confirmation then becomes an adult rite of joining the church and of owning their faith, not the "gate to Communion" that it is at present.

- When adults comment that "children don't understand", I query how many of us understand this means of grace? And why should an adult's understanding be more desirable than that of a child? What about adults with learning difficulties?

- The experience of churches that have allowed children to receive has been very positive, both in terms of the children growing up and remaining within the worshipping community, and in mission terms towards those families and others.

- Within the terms of an intergenerational community, excluding the children from Communion is oxymoronic.

Preparation of the adults

I remember asking at a job interview, in spring 2001, whether this church admitted children to Communion prior to their confirmation. A very definite "no" was the answer. I had in my previous post worked hard to deliver Communion prior to confirmation to the children of that parish, so had already rehearsed the delicate task of persuading adults to enable this practice as a great step forward for the whole church.[3]

The first step was to put this into the aims and objectives for the church, four years down the line – aiming for 2005. This was a church that had not had a mission statement with "aims and objectives" so the whole thing was a bit of a jolt. People only tended to notice the immediate objectives, which included lowering the average age of the PCC. Some thought this meant I was going to murder them in their beds to open up vacancies, so by the time we'd assured them that it was not so, objectives for several years hence were not being taken in.

As the years went by, people started to read what I'd planned with the wardens and PCC for more than a year ahead, and so conversations began about the whole idea of allowing children to receive. Once people had got over the "I didn't so why should they" moment, they discovered what a good idea it was. So as 2005 drew closer, we scheduled some specific content for the PCC of that year:

- To discuss what Communion means for each of us;

- To discuss baptism;

- To discuss confirmation.

This series of discussions was very helpful and took place in a very positive spirit.

The diocesan children's officer had sent me a "what to do" pack, and we continued to follow the instructions according to diocesan guidelines.

We then invited the diocesan children's officer to convene a meeting for the whole parish. We also invited the incumbent of a parish where children had been receiving Communion for several years, to share how it had affected the church. This meeting was well publicized:

- Everyone attending any service for the preceding month received a paper flier.

- A substantial article was placed in the parish magazine.

- It was advertised in the notices every week for the previous month.

- It was also advertised in our paper pew notices every week for the previous month.

The meeting was well attended, and our children's officer was very good. She took us through the history of this matter, and then the visiting incumbent told us about his church's experience. The dialogue was very healthy, and the advisory vote at the end of the meeting well in favour. The PCC voted at the next meeting 19-1 in favour. The next stage was to write to the bishop of the diocese asking for his permission to proceed. We had to send back the checklist from the guidelines including information about how we would prepare the children. We had, along the way, purchased a couple of schemes, but once we received permission, my curate and I sat down together and made up our own, to suit our children and our context. (Off the shelf courses are great, but some tinkering is always needed to ensure you get what you really want.)

The course[4]

A key factor with this enterprise is involving parents/carers with the children. Every child needs to be supported through this process, for the sake of both the child and the church, and it's also an excellent tool for mission and education back home!

We therefore sent out a letter to every child that we could think of who was even vaguely part of the church.[5] This included the Sunday school, the choir, all the children who came to church affiliated groups, and so on, inviting parents and children to a meeting after church one Sunday to discuss the possibility of their children receiving Communion prior to confirmation. At that meeting, if the family was interested, they could pick up an application form, listing details of the planned course dates and times and a tear-off application form.[6]

In my present diocese, the youngest age for this scheme is seven.[7] Our first cohort of children included three seven-year-olds, and then rose to a couple of thirteen-year olds, who would be confirmed later that year anyway. We also included a six-year-old, who had two older siblings in the course. They came from a very supportive family, all sang in the choir, and their mum was on the PCC, so I had no qualms in including her.

The course began with sixteen children, divided into two groups. We had hoped that the older children would group together, but they didn't, so both groups had the full age span, which was not ideal for them, but they proved very helpful with the younger ones!

We allowed five sessions prior to the service, then another at the end, which became a real celebratory event for the whole church community.

The course was based around the structure of the Communion/Eucharist service as follows:

- **Week 1**: Beginning/gathering;
- **Week 2**: Belonging/word/story;
- **Week 3**: Belonging in baptism/creed;
- **Week 4**: Story of the last supper/dinner. Remembering and sharing/Eucharistic prayer;
- **Week 5**: Sending out.

Essential kit

For each child we purchased:

- A school-type exercise book. The modern words of the "Lord's Prayer" were stuck in the inside cover;
- A pencil;

- A plastic book bag to keep the book and pencil safe;
- Lots of stickers.

Every week we came with a large themed outline for the child to write the week's prayer into. These were stuck into the exercise books, along with the homework sheet.

The course took place in church. We set up a working area (tables, chairs, and so on) in one of our side aisles that is not usually needed for worship. We also had a large area of display boards ready to add to every week. On this we had a large outline of the church. The congregation were encouraged to look at this display as it logged our progress weekly. We had a flip chart ready in the working area. (This was before many churches had projectors and screens, and in this circumstance, I think the old-fashioned approach may be better.)

You will also need lots of glue sticks, colouring kits, and various other craft supplies. We always had at least two adults working behind the scenes with us.

On the Sunday before we began, all the children were listed in our weekly notice sheet. During the service, we brought them out and committed the whole church to praying for them as we travelled down through the weeks together.

Week 1: gathering – exploring church

Set up: A treasure trail is laid around the church. It ends at the altar/Lord's table. On the altar are the children's books, folders, pencils, and pieces of paper (three names per A4 size) for their names.

You need a outline of your church almost as large as a page in the exercise books, one for each child, and a note for each child of the homework for this week.

1. Begin by welcoming the children.

2. Explain how the treasure hunt works: We gave them the first clue, then when they arrived at that place the next clue was read out to the whole group, and so on. This keeps the

smaller ones with the faster ones and ensures that they all end together at the altar/Lord's table. Run through what each place you have been to is for. What is the point of the pews? What is the lectern for? Why do we have an altar/table?

3. At the altar, you will find the books etc. Hand out one of each per child and lead them back to the working area.

4. Each child now writes their name on the piece of paper and decorates it as they wish. (These need to be laminated before the next session.)

5. Each child is given the prayer outline for the week, which they stick into their book.

6. Discuss with the children what would they like as their prayer this week? This is a prayer that we compose together (try to keep it down to one sentence). Write it onto the flip chart, and then each child writes it into their prayer outline.

7. Each child is given seven stickers and told that every day they need to pray the prayer with an adult, and then they stick a sticker for each day into their prayer outline.

8. Explain their homework: Bring in a photo or picture of themselves, ideally with other members of their family, to be included in the developing display in church. They can also use their books to record how life is for them, like a diary or a journal, but that's optional.

9. Ask each child to quietly go to a place in the church that they regard as particularly holy, where they will feel close to God. Spend a few moments in quiet, the children with their eyes closed and just focusing on that place. Say a clear "amen" so they know when the prayer time is finished, and then make sure they have their folders and everything inside that should be there before they go home.

Week 2: word/story – the Good Shepherd

Set up: This week's content is based around the Good Shepherd story from Godly Play.[8] Don't underestimate the amount of time it will take you to learn the session and to organize the materials; this is not a last minute session! I used the chancel space to tell the story; you will need a suitable quiet space with enough room for the children to sit comfortably in a circle.

This week's prayer outline is that of a sheep. One per child.

Their names will have been laminated. You will need Blu Tack or similar to attach them to the display.

Art/craft materials need to be laid out at the working area.

1. Welcome the children.

2. Talk through their homework – look at the photographs and so on and ask the helpers to attach them to the display. Let the children put their names up on the display.

3. Tell the story. Spend plenty of time wondering with them.

4. Ask them to do some work, reflecting on how the story made them feel. They return to the working area one at a time and the helpers set up each child with materials. Once each child has finished their piece of work, let them place it in the display – if they want to. Some may need to take them home to finish.

5. About seven minutes from the end, move on to this week's prayer. Write it on the flip chart as they suggest what they would like to pray about this week. The children write it into their outline. (We found it easiest if the helpers stuck these outlines into the children's books during the storytelling.)

6. Distribute this week's stickers and homework sheet.

7. Say the prayer together.

Week 3: belonging/baptism

Set up: You need a small doll or teddy to baptize. Use the font or have a bowl of water. Bring a towel.

The prayer outline this week is of a candle. One per child.

You will also need a badge machine. Most dioceses/area youth offices will be able to lend you one of these. They can be the very difficult to use – have a practice first!

Get your church's baptism register and have it ready to look at.

1. Welcome the children.

2. Look at the mementoes of their baptism that they have brought, (part of last week's homework). Some of them may remember being baptized – if so encourage them to share. Some of the older ones may remember the baptisms of some of the youngest – encourage them to reminisce together.

3. Look in the baptism register for the names of the children who are present.

4. Take the children through a baptism, using the doll. Use the "I wonder" formula that you used with Godly Play last week. Then chat about how adults are baptized – one of your helpers may like to experience this again!

5. Baptism is about joining the church, belonging to the church. Back at the work area, let each child design and make a badge about belonging to God/the church. Ideally, make two copies of each, so that the second is added to the display.

6. Distribute this week's stickers and homework sheet.

7. Write this week's prayer.

Week 4: story of the Last Supper

Set up: This week's story is the Godly Play retelling of the Jesus' last Passover[9] or Jesus and the twelve,[10] Make sure you order/make the visual aids in plenty of time, so you can practise.

I also used some pitta bread and very watery wine. Check with all parents/carers that it's OK to give their children bread and wine before the session. The prayer outline is of a chalice.

Note: The word "supper" is not common parlance with children. You may need to explain this meal. Several of my children call this celebration "Jesus' last dinner".

1. Welcome the children. If they have lots of energy, play a quick game of "where's this place" using the correct names for parts of the building, such as lectern, pulpit, Lady Chapel, and so on.

2. Calm the children and then lead them to the Godly Play space. I used the altar/Lord's table in church to tell this, with the children standing in a circle around the table. You may prefer to be seated on the floor with them.

3. Tell them the story. If you are using real pitta and wine, hand it round at the appropriate point in the story.

4. Give the children time to wonder, then go to the work area one at a time to do some work based on how the story made them feel. If they finish in time, and they want to, they can add their work to the display. Some may need to finish at home.

5. Devise the prayer for this week. Say the prayer together.

6. Give out the stickers and homework sheet for this week.

Week 5: sending out – journeying together/ mission possible

Set up: Each child will need an empty matchbox. You also need to prepare the work cards to illustrate the structure of the Eucharist, and how it's been reflected in the course. You will need the vessels that are used to distribute Communion, with the cloths that cover them.

The prayer outline this week is of a circle of people holding hands.

1. Welcome the children. Give each one a matchbox and challenge them to scour the church to find as many things as they can to put in their matchbox.

2. Compare the contents. Explain that we sent them on a mission that sounded very hard (we have such a clean church) but they managed to find all these things. What do they think our mission is as Christians?

3. Using the work cards, work through the course, thinking about it in terms of where it is reflected the Communion service:

- Gathering (treasure hunt, journey, beginning);

- Word (story, parable, learning);

- Creed (baptism, belief, peace, church as a family);

- Eucharistic prayer (remembering and sharing the last dinner);

- Add this session – sending out (continuing the journey).

This leads onto the Eucharist liturgy. Take a picture of one part of the service, and find a separate card with the word to name that part of the service, such as "gathering". Have a word card with a matching picture for every part of the service. Now put them together and in the correct order.

4. Stress how important it is for them to keep going – to be a Christian we need to be sustained by church and share together, and so on.

5. To break up the words, play a quick game. Run to where:

- We sit in church (will vary, mainly the nave);

- We hear story/Bible/sermon;
- Baptize people (at this point, check their understanding – belief in triune God).

Then:

- Demonstrate how we greet each other in the middle of the service (shake hands);
- Ask where the Last Supper/dinner is re-enacted. Go to the altar rail and practise receiving Communion using the vessels they will use "on the day";
- Ask what happens at the end of the service ("Go in peace to love and serve the Lord");
- Write the prayer for the week. Ask the children how we serve God out in the world and use that to build the prayer.

Week 6: the celebration

This is for after the children have received their first Communion.

Set up: Make sure the display is clearly visible. Organize whatever refreshments are going to be available. Have certificates ready.

This session had no formal structure. It is important that all the church is invited, perhaps to share a meal together, and to talk with the children about why they wanted to receive, and how they felt now that they had achieved that aim. The children can all be given a personalized certificate to mark the occasion.

It is also important to thank the members of the church for the support that they have extended to the children.

It is required that you note down the names of the children who receive, along with the date, in your parish confirmation book for future record.

* * *

Clearly, this course was devised for our church, at our time. Next time it will be different; use your initiative to fit a course for the group that you have, and enjoy!

If you want to run such a course as intergenerational, and many adults come into faith through their children's involvement with church and may want to undertake a preparatory course with their children, then this is the structure I recommend:

The whole course is taught through Godly Play stories.[11] After the story, only the children wonder out loud – ask the adults to hold their thoughts inside. Once you move to the creative response, split the group into children and adults and set the children off on their work. Let the adults sit and share their wondering, with creative materials and Play-Doh to facilitate as they talk together.

The stories for the course are as follows. For details of how Godly Play works, see chapter 8 in this book, and do go on at least a "taster" session before trying to use Godly Play.

- **Week 1**: Creation[12]

- **Week 2**: The Holy Family.[13]

- **Week 3**: The Good Shepherd.[14]

- **Week 4**: Jesus' Last Passover.[15]

- **Week 5**: The Circle of the Eucharist.[16]

You will also need to ensure that everyone involved has been baptized/christened. If they have not, then arrange to baptize them before they receive Communion together.

I am convinced that the intergenerational method is preferable to adults and children undergoing the same course separately – and think of all the child sitting it saves if the course for the adults has been done in the evenings and they come out without their children!

Modern families like to do things together in their very precious free time, so what better use of that time than to grow as Christians together.

Questions for discussion

1. How do you think your church would view allowing children to receive Communion prior to confirmation?

2. Where do our attitudes towards receiving Communion come from? Perhaps you could share your earliest memories and see if you can trace those very strong feelings that you have about this.

3. What benefit do you see for the children, and their families, through allowing children to receive in this way?

4. How would this affect your church?

Appendix 1

Time, space, story, ritual: a year of Godly Play

This work arose as part of my post as Faith and Nurture Adviser for the Diocese of Canterbury. This was an experimental position with a three-year contract, designed to try and bring together churches, schools, and families, with the focus on the worshipping child.[1] Part of the post was to conduct some research, and this paper is the result of that work. It has been included here as an illustration of how powerful Godly Play can be when used well in after school clubs. It also addresses the question of the benefit of a designated Godly Play space.

My work was overseen by Rebecca Nye. Originally, I wanted to look for evidence of developing spirituality, but Rebecca pointed out that spirituality is impossible to measure – how would it "develop"? She was more concerned that, as the children grew older, their latent spirituality was still there and observable. So all my enthusiastic outcomes were put to one side, and all I did was to watch, listen, and record. Inevitably, I became more than an observer, as curious children wanted to know what I was writing down in my book, and I developed relationships with the lovely children that grew to become a regular part of my life for a year. Both schools in the study are church schools in a wealthy area of Kent. Both clubs were run by Godly Play three-day trained facilitators. One school, Colliers Green, has a designated Godly Play room. The other, Goudhurst, was meeting in a classroom space. Both groups were using Godly Play, devised by Jerome Berryman from many strands of Christian education, with Montessori principles.

Rebecca and I spoke for a good while on how to measure or even account for what is essentially a very personal experience – that of spirituality and evidence of spirituality being shared. She shared with me this amazingly helpful expression: a MOG (Moment of Ordinary Grace), which is a transitory experience – a pause, full of meaning, a deep silence, where all are watching and waiting, a pause which could go on forever. You cannot measure it, or quantify it in any way, but it indicated the children's spirituality being fully present for me. It is a subtle moment, a pause, a breath, but I frequently experience this myself, and when I'm leading Godly Play my internal self knows that we're ready now – we've arrived, ready to explore the story together. A MEG (Moment of Exceptional Grace) is when a larger group shares the moment, such as collective worship in school, or when a group is out at night, looking at the stars.

So, to the research.

Time

I observed the groups for a minimum of ten sessions each. The Colliers Green group ran for an hour, Goudhurst ran for 45 minutes. Both groups met on a weekly basis. While the relationships between facilitators and children were excellent, supporting adult/child relationships varied. Critically, part way through the research, Goudhurst moved to lunchtime, 30 minutes, with a different adult (teacher) in charge, which changed again when the local church appointed a new families minister, who was not Godly Play trained. Whilst the changes at Goudhurst meant that research conditions changed, in that the content was now nearer to a traditional Sunday school in an English church, it became fascinating to see the effect on the children, and how the group, now renamed "Trinity Lights", became younger and larger. The most obvious move was that it became more learning objective led rather than an exploratory session – the feeling was that the adults were teaching the children rather than exploring together on a far more egalitarian footing.

When I spoke afterwards with three girls who stopped coming after the change, they said they had enjoyed the interactive nature of the Godly Play group and doing the drama together at the end and found the repeat of the stories "interesting". They had been attending for three years, two of which focused on Godly Play. They didn't attend now because of other activities at the same time, and the increased number of children meant less time for each person to relate within the group. When talking about Godly Play as opposed to the Trinity Lights activities one said, "You enter into the story more fully" with Godly Play. When asked about hearing the story more than once, two girls referred to the actual resource varying (a river could be represented by ribbon one time, and wool the next) but one also said that sometimes "what they were talking about to you" also changed, for instance, the meaning. Interestingly, she felt there was an agenda, something "you should have learned" behind both the Godly Play and Trinity Lights.

Space

"The Ark", Colliers Green's designated Godly Play space, represents a huge investment by the facilitator, David Gillies, at that time also a school governor and worship leader.

Whilst I was familiar with a designated Godly Play classroom, I hadn't seen one being used before and the impact of the room was part of my learning. David is retired and a lay minister in the local church. He leads the school worship as well as the group, so is familiar to all the children. The room makes all the stories within the Godly Play curriculum available to all of the children for their private response time, thus, they can access and retell stories, work with the sand of the desert bag, or just be quiet. No one tells them what to do, and new members of the group soon learn. All response materials are available all the time – including the "desert bag", always the first resource that the children would ask to work with. The room and its design appear to facilitate flow, and those working in the sand were often working subconsciously, frequently creating and building. Most often they were rehearsing funeral rites ("Abraham died and was buried..."). Others drew, painted, and chatted quietly. I recognized that the environment positively influences the children's participation and spirituality; the calm environment, and the knowledge that the Ark is their own space, gave a freedom and joy to the children's time within the group.

Working within such a space allows children to make sensorial links among all of the images and means of Christian communication.

Jerome Berryman[2]

The children worked in small groups or in parallel, while the others happily set to, on their own, but frequently chatting as they worked. Children reworking previous stories worked alone, occasionally talking to themselves, usually retelling the story. Sometimes they went to their work folders and looked through previous work and added to it. Several times the children sang as they worked, usually started by one child. They sang folk songs that they must have been singing in school, and they sang with joy and a reflective note which bound the group as one but allowed them to work independently. I found this deeply moving, and indicative of a profound comfort in the room as well as a surfacing of their creativity and spirituality. It was a form of MOG for me, and I think for them too. The room was facilitating this spontaneous expression of joy, as it contributed through the total safety that they felt.

The Goudhurst group met in the music room; quite small, including (upright) piano and various storage areas, but lower numbers facilitated easier working. Outside space was used for response time when weather permitted. There was also access to a neighbouring practice room, often used when the children devised a short drama as their collective response. Unlike the Godly Play room at Colliers Green, children at Goudhurst didn't have access to other Godly Play stories to work with, just paper and coloured pencils to draw or write with. They often went into the practice room together to make up a drama, usually with the same child organizing them. This meant that individual children may not have been able to work on what the story is saying to them, just the larger group experience, dominated by the self selected "director".

If we can only wait, [the patient] arrives at understanding creatively and with immense joy... The principle is that it is the patient, and only the patient who has the answers.

Donald Winnicott[3]

Despite the limitations, the quality of thinking and working going on within this group was very high. Kev, the facilitator, was a patient listener and clearly valued each child and their contribution. Some profound comments came from this group.

Wonderings 1

Child 2: Talking about this, would a normal shepherd care for them? Or would no one care about them...
If the ordinary shepherd cared about them, but we didn't have a Good Shepherd, just an ordinary one?

Kev (KD): Yeah, what if we didn't have a Good Shepherd, just ordinary ones, and no one cared for the sheep. What would happen then?

CO (teacher): Very interesting question, what if there was no Good Shepherd, just ordinary shepherds?

KD: It would be a very different place, wouldn't it? This whole place would be very different, cos the ordinary shepherd, when it was dangerous, just ran away. When the wolf came, he didn't hang around.

Child 2: Cos he didn't show them the way, the Good Shepherd did.

KD: The ordinary shepherd didn't show them the way, he didn't know them by name. The Good Shepherd knew each of the sheep with their funny names – he knew all those funny names, didn't he? That's interesting. That's a really good question, good thinking. Perhaps you'd like to think about that as you play.

Child 2 murmurs

Child 1: Didn't we have a wolf character last time?

KD: Yes, we had a wolf character last time. You'll have to imagine him this time.

Child 1: Did the wolf get lost?

KD: He got chased away by the Good Shepherd, shooed him away.

Wondering together at the end of the story invites the listeners to explore where they are in that story today. The wondering questions are carefully arranged, taking the listeners more deeply into the essence of the story. One of the questions often used is "What could we take away and still have everything we need for the story?" An example of what the children said is outlined below.

Wonderings 2

Child 1: When the shepherds came.

David Gillies (DG): You think we could take that away... ah-ha. Shepherds were... they were... they weren't like the magi, they were ordinary people, so perhaps they were important as representing us? Just a thought... Yes?

Child 3: I think we should take away... the ox, I mean, him just looking into his bed and seeing the baby there instead, take out the baby from the manger, so he can have his food! Change the story.

DG: I see, so we should change the story? Aah. I don't think we can do that.

Child 3: But the ox has an apple core.

DG: I think we have to stick with the story, think about what can be taken away, not changed...

Child 5: Either Mary or the donkey, but we can't change the story. It kind of changes the story. Like every single person or bit tells part of the story, they're all the same. The story is like it is. If we take something away, we change the story.

DG: I think that's very clever of you to see that. The story is, is like it is, and you can't take anything away without completely changing it, so I don't think you can take things away. Yes?

Child 4: I would take away one of the Magi, only one.

DG: Only one? Do you mind which one?

Child 4: So which one gave him gold?

DG: This one.

Child 4: Frankincense then. And myrrh. Take away myrrh then.

DG: That's a very smelly herb.

Child 4: Smelly?

DG: Mm. It's got a very strong smell. When you've taken him away, wouldn't you have changed the story, don't you think?

Child 4: It is how it is (shrugs), that's his life.

DG: In ancient times, and still today, we think of gold as a most wonderful present, just the thing to give to a king. We don't so much now, but in olden times, frankincense was bound up with the idea of worship, this person being important and so I worship them, and myrrh was used when people died, so in a way, all three presents are quite important. Gold for a king, frankincense to worship God and myrrh because... he died.

Child 4: But he's not going to die anytime soon! He could just pick them up from the ground!

DG: Don't you think that's the wonderful bit about the story? It's looking forward, you're quite right, he's not going to die yet... not for ages!

Child 4: He's not going to die soon... then you don't get the chance to use it!

Child 5: I think I would take out the grown-up Jesus.[4]

DG: Wow! You'd take out the grown-up Jesus?

Child 5: He's a baby! He can't be a baby and turn into a grown up.

Child 6: It's the spirit…

DG: No, you can't, and that's a clever thing you said because we are telling the story, but we're also looking forward, not to the end of the story, but to the point when Jesus isn't on the earth any more.

Child 2: I've got another one.

DG: We're looking at the beginning, and the end.

Child 2: Maybe we could take out one of the sheep? (Giggles)

DG: There were lots of sheep, and we've only got two anyway, but they do represent sheep, they're to remind you that the shepherd was looking after, the shepherds, cos there were lots of them were looking after lots of sheep.

Child 1: Erm, I don't think you can take anything out cos if you did, it wouldn't be right any more.

DG: I think you're right.

Wonderings 3

Perhaps the most interesting dialogue about leaving out part of the story occurred towards the end of my observations, after the story of Ruth:

DG: Which bit of the story do you think you could take away and still have everything that we need?

Child 4: I think we could take away… like… them two.

Child 2 and 7: But then you wouldn't have the same story!

Child 7: You wouldn't have Jesus.

Child 4: That's not part of this story.

Child 7: (Quite irate) *But then you wouldn't have Jesus because his dad wouldn't have been born!*

Child 2: Basically, you can't take anything away because then you'd have… it would be a different story!

Child 6: Actually, I think you could take away like, erm, this bit (the field).

Chorus: No!

Child 6: You could take away this person, and some more, but still have Joseph and then you'd still have Jesus, like you could take out this person.

Child 2: But then she wouldn't be a great-grandmother.

Child 5: It doesn't matter.

DG: It can't be quite right, because if we took away your daddy, and we had someone else as your daddy, we wouldn't have you, we'd have someone quite different. You have to have each one, in each age, to make the line go on and on and on and get the people that you want.

Child 4: And then he couldn't marry the one that he was supposed to marry, because…

Child 6: You could take away him.

DG: Boaz?

Child 6: And you could stop them dying.

Laughter

Child 4: The father, make him still alive.

Child 5: If anything was taken out, they'd be different, because everyone is important, like everyone is making it, if it wasn't important they wouldn't have written it down just for the sake of it.

Child 3: Take away one of the dead people.

Child 5: But the crops, they're important because that's what, that's how they came across Boaz and that's how they had the children, they had in the end became Jesus. If you took away the house they wouldn't live there.

Child 6: But they had a house this side or that side in the beginning.

Child 2: But if you took away one single person you wouldn't have you... If you took away one single person, it would stop the whole of man. If you took away the person at the very start...

DG: Naomi?

Child 2: Yes, or her husband, then... erm... it would stop the whole entire line cos they wouldn't have been able to have children.

Child 4: You could take away that building

DG: What, Bethlehem?!

Child 2: They'd have nowhere to go apart from Moab!

Child 6: And Jesus wouldn't have been born.

Child 4: That's just a castle!

DG: It's a town. "O little town of Bethlehem."

Child 2: This is this. It's different but it's the same thing. It's not the right story at all.

DG: OK, OK.

Child 2: Jesus would be different.

During this exchange, Child 2 was becoming quite irate, and emotional. She was not prepared to let the story change, because she really seems to have understood the place of this story in salvation history. Child 2 is about nine years old. Godly Play is based upon a three-year "spiral curriculum", and it is clear some children have experienced some stories several times. Some stories are repeated: "The Holy Family" is repeated every time the liturgical colour changes. The theory is that children hear, learn, and then inhabit the story.

This spiral curriculum was evident in the children at Goudhurst in particular. Two of the older children had attended since the onset of the Thursday Club, and so had heard some of the stories several times. This was underlined when I heard them saying verbatim the script to the "mustard seed" parable when this story was looked at at a Trinity Lights session. They recognized that there was different learning/meaning each time and they found that interesting. (They are both regular church attendees, and I wonder if they may have heard the "official" "what the story means" at Sunday groups there.)

> What is revealed to infants – and to young children
> generally – is then revealed by them, at least to those with
> the humility to notice what these little ones are telling
> them.
>
> **John Pridmore**[5]

Thus, the Godly Play session is a time of learning for all in the room – not just the children.

Story

Wonderings 4

This is a comment that one of the older girls made during the wondering about the disciples:

DG: *Tell me which one you don't like, and you're not allowed to say Judas because everyone would say Judas and it would become rather...* (Grimaced expressions from the group.) *Oh, alright, you can say Judas!*

(After quite a long series of "Judas" answers)

Child 5: *I don't think there are any bad ones. Like, even Judas, he followed Jesus, and maybe something bad happened and forced him out to do it or something? I don't know much about it, but something could have happened and he just, might have just forgotten about it, just for a moment? I know that's not right, but I don't think any of them should be disliked, cos they're all following Jesus, in a way, so they're all helping to tell the story?*

DG: *They certainly helped to tell the story, that's absolutely true. I can't quite go along with your very generous view of Judas.*

Child 5: *I don't know much about him.*

DG: *Because, well, we don't know much, and we certainly aren't told about any special circumstances, but what we are told is that he was really disappointed with himself, so if his wife had been terribly ill, and he simply had to betray Jesus to get some money to make her better, I don't think he'd have felt so bad about it himself, but he did.*

Child 5: *"I'm not bothered, I'm going to betray Jesus," he could have done that.*

DG: *Yes, he could. Most of us read the story as him doing something very much for himself, the story tends to portray him as a bit of a thief, a bit of a sneaky thief.*

Child 5: *But they don't know that – they could write what they want, he doesn't know what the truth is.*

DG: *Hmmm, OK, that's not wrong, that's not wrong, people do write things that are not true and they're not true and they're not correct.*

Child 5: *They could have been a bit right, not like on the point, not exactly on the point, so they didn't say why Judas betrayed Jesus.*

According to Godly Play theory, as well as good practice, there are always two adults in the room – the storyteller and the doorkeeper.

At the end of each session it is recommended that they reflect together as to how the story and the session has impacted on them. At Colliers Green, I was able to do this with David, but at Goudhurst, Kev was usually hurrying off to family duties, and we weren't able to share in this way.

One striking moment at Colliers Green was when a new doorkeeper, a teacher, came for the first time. At the end of the session she simply asked, "How did you get them to talk like that? I've never heard those children speak that way before." I am still musing over some of the conversations that I heard, and the transactions that I witnessed.

Ritual

Godly Play sessions are based upon a Eucharistic service:

- Arrival
- Greeting
- Story
- Reflection
- Response
- Feast/sharing
- Sending out

> *Godly Play contrasts talking about Scripture and worship with being in Scripture and worship.*

Jerome Berryman[6]

This structure may not be clear to the casual observer, but to the children it gave great security. Indeed, when the wondering conversations went on for too long (we had little time left before the parents/carers arrived), we occasionally had to leave out the creative responses, and that caused great outcry. Greater outcry, however, would have been heard if we had missed out "The Feast" at Colliers Green, as one of the mums sent in home-made brownies every week for this, and the children fell upon this treat! But the children waited for their feast; after clearing creative work away, children gave out napkins, a brownie, and water to each child, and they said a prayer before devouring this delicious feast.

John Pridmore, the great Godly Play advocate, wrote the following in his stunning book, *Playing with Icons:*

> *It is at this boundary between land and sea, between* **here** *where we are safe, and* **there** *where, most certainly, we are not safe, children play.*[7]

For some people Godly Play is threatening, as adults are not controlling the direction, the learning, or the outcomes. Pridmore recognizes the risky place that we may travel to if we allow children to demonstrate and lead us in their extraordinary contact with their spirituality. Godly Play is not safe.

So, at the end of a year, what did I learn?

- Large numbers of MOGs witnessed;

- Extraordinary wisdom coming from the mouths of children;

- Inclusion of all participants;

- Profound relationships between the children and the adults;

- Children exploring existential questions freely and with integrity;

- "Troubled" children working towards peace;

- Adults being profoundly changed by their interaction with the children.

In Canterbury diocese, we have a policy named "fellow pilgrims" in which we acknowledge our belief that adults don't have a greater access to spirituality than children, but rather we travel through life with children by our sides, and that learning and experiences are gained as there is a two-way recognition of what one brings to the other. Watching, listening, and thinking about what I saw and heard profoundly changed me; the gift of the work was the joy and overflowing spirituality of the children in their Godly Play sessions, and this challenged me to challenge others to listen to what children bring, even as we withdraw up the beach with our deckchairs and laptops.

Appendix 2

Creative Christmas

This appendix, a creative and informal act of intergenerational worship, is taken from the report back to the PCC after the event took place. It is included to give a practical example of what such an event might entail.

29 November 2018, 11 a.m. – 2 p.m.
Aim: To offer an informal creative Christmas event,
with Messy Church values, open to all ages.
Creativity, hospitality, and worship.
£5 donation suggested.
Set up from 9.30 a.m.

Crafts team

- Christmas card making
- Décopatch decorations
- Table decorations
- Glass tea light holders
- Bark slice decorations
- Poppy head angels
- Play-Doh table and area for children's toys
- Christmas music in church
- Tables set up in church
- Tablecloths
- Tables in link to place creations on

Food and kitchen team

- Beef casserole
- Spicy sausage casserole
- Vegetarian shepherd's pie (GF)
- Pasta, tomato sauce and cheese
- Pasta
- Rice
- Bread rolls and butter
- Green salad
- Mince pies, chocolate brownies, cream
- GF mince pies
- Petit Filous fromage frais
- Celebration chocolates
- Tables set up to seat forty, plus a children's table

Post-event feedback

- Attendance: Approximately thirty-seven including six children;
- Singing carols and a two minute welcome and Christmas homily was well received;
- Positive feedback from everyone;
- Timing was good;
- We borrowed Christmas tablecloths, battery tea lights, and light up tree, which were great.

To improve:
- One meat and one vegetarian dish is plenty;
- Rice cooked better than pasta in large quantities;
- A couple of French sticks sliced would be plenty;
- More help for clearing up at the end;
- Suggestion of a six-sided snowflake craft.

Were our aims achieved?

Yes. We had a whole mix of ages who came together, from a newborn baby with mum, mums and toddlers, grandmas and grandchildren, to twenties, and older people in their seventies and eighties. There was a mix of people from the regular church community and others who had never been to Lawford church before.

The atmosphere was friendly and sociable with children and adults creating and chatting alongside one other. New friendships were made.

The hot lunch was very well received and provided another opportunity to create community. It was a good environment for carols and to pause to reflect on Christmas just for a short time.

All in all the event was positive and provides a building block from which another "Creative" event could take place.

Thanks to Gill and Simon Heron, from St Mary's Lawford in Chelmsford diocese, for sharing this account.

Notes

Introduction

1. Lamont, R., *Understanding Children Understanding* God (London: SPCK, 2007).

2. I'm using Sunday school as the name of what churches provide for children and young people; I know there are many, more exciting names used.

3. This is not so for some people with learning difficulties, who may not move out of their childish thinking.

4. Berryman, J. W., *Godly Play* (Minneapolis, MN: Augsburg Fortress, 1991).

Chapter 1

1. Hay, D. and R. Nye, *The Spirit of the Child* (London: Fount, 1998).

2. I use "sin" as an example as it seems to me that most people outside the church, and those who are regarded as "fringe members", may have a very limited understanding of what "sin" means. It is not often heard in the vernacular any longer in this country, and even within the church, understanding of this concept is sometimes very limited.

3. I have heard it said that 100 per cent of the population have had a spiritual experience, quoting David Hay's research. My personal thinking is that not everyone but most people have had such an experience.

4. It is, of course, possible to talk about God without being spiritual. Those reading for a degree in theology, philosophy, or other similar degrees will debate God for hours, in a purely academic way. We each have our own, unique concept of God, no matter the type of background from which we come, much as I have a concept of Disneyland without experiencing the reality.

5. This is very noticeable when an interviewer tackles people such as highly regarded political commentators; they often relate to their spirituality with a very child-like understanding, which communicates as peculiarly out of step with their clearly well-advanced, adult, intellectual thinking.

6. Wordsworth, W., *Ode on Intimations of Immortality from Recollections of Early Childhood*: https://www.bartleby.com/101/536.html (last accessed 12 February 2019).

7. Loder, J., *The Transforming Moment* (Colorado Springs: Helmers and Howard, 1989).

8. For a recent research example of this see Sorea, D. and F. Scârneci-Domnişoru, "Unorthodox Depictions of Divinity: Romanian children's drawings of Him, Her or It," *The International Journal of Children's Spirituality*, Vol 23, 4, 2018.

9. See Hay, D and R. Nye, *The Spirit of the Child*, for more detail.

10. Peggy Way refers to the "ordinary grace" that places "ultimacy and immediacy in the same sentence." See Way, P., *Created by God: Pastoral Care for All God's People* (St. Louis: Chalice Press, 2005), pp. 41-42.

Chapter 3

1. This is particularly clear with children who have a Symbol spiritual style – see chapter 4.
2. Toddler training books recommend the following: when the child cries, wait for five minutes, then go in and stroke the child, but do not lift them from their bed/cot. Say a few calming words, then leave the room. Keep repeating every five minutes. We had sleepless nights for two years, tried this, and it worked the first night, after fifteen minutes/three visits. It's very, very hard, so parents are usually quite desperate by the time they do it, and this will give them the willpower to manage the strategy.
3. Myers-Briggs tables taken from Watts, Nye and Savage, *Psychology for Christian Ministry* (Abingdon: Routledge, 2002). Used with permission.
4. There are, of course, more stages in Erikson's scheme – do look at them if this has caught your interest. For example, Watts, F., R. Nye and S. Savage, *Psychology for Christian Ministry*, p.107.

Chapter 4

1. Associate Professor of Lay Empowerment and Discipleship at McMaster Divinity College, McMaster University, Hamilton, Ontario, Canada.
2. In 2009, PhD student at Union Theological Seminary and Presbyterian School of Christian Education, Richmond, Virginia, USA.
3. The children were aged seven to eleven.
4. Csinos, D., *Children's Ministry that Fits* (Eugene, OR: Wipf and Stock, 2011) Used by permission of Wipf and Stock Publishers. www.wipfandstock.com.
5. From the Introduction in Csinos, D., *Children's Ministry that Fits*.

Chapter 5

1. This is very common within a church context and something to be aware of.
2. Spiritual styles may inform what was going on, but this was long before David Csinos was even born.
3. *School of Rock*, directed by Linklater (Hollywood, CA: Paramount, 2003).
4. Especially "Stairway to Heaven" on Led Zeppelin, *Led Zeppelin IV*, Atlantic Records, 1971.
5. Golding, W., *The Lord of the Flies* (London: Faber and Faber, 1954).
6. Sopel, J., *If Only They Didn't Speak English* (London: BBC Books, 2018).
7. Harding, J., *One Big Damn Puzzler* (London: Black Swan, 2006).
8. Schaffer, H. R., *The Child's Entry into a Social World* (London: Academic Press, 1984).
9. See https://allpoetry.com/No-man-is-an-island.
10. Bowlby, J., "The nature of the child's tie to his mother," *International Journal of Psychoanalysis*, 39 (1958), pp.1-23.
11. Feshbach, N. D., "Empathy, Empathy Training and the Regulation of Aggression in Elementary School Children," in Kaplan, R.M. (Ed.), *Aggression in Children and Youth* (Basel: Springer, 1984), pp. 192-208.

12. Codrington, G. and S. Grant-Marshall, *Mind the Gap* (London: Fig Tree, 2011).

Chapter 6

1. Fowler divides our faith life into six distinct stages. For more detail, see Fowler, J. W., *Stages of Faith* (San Francisco: Harper Collins, 1995).

2. Fowler's research began with interviews with children who were four years old. Comments regarding younger children are deduced from cognitive development theory and observation.

3. See Rizzuto, A-M., *The Birth of the Living God* (Chicago: University of Chicago Press, 1979).

4. Now working at King Alfred's College, University of Winchester.

5. There are some fabulous pictures of children's ideas about God in Sorea, D. and F. Scârneci-Domnişoru, "Unorthodox Depictions of Divinity: Romanian children's drawings of Him, Her or It," *The International Journal of Children's Spirituality*, Vol 23, 4, 2018.

6. There are three more stages of faith, but they do not fall within the scope of this book. If you would like to read more about them and reflect on what Fowler has to say, most ministers have some of his work on their bookshelves, and there may be a local minister who has studied Fowler in depth who can help. I recommend the General Synod Board of Education's *How Faith Grows* (London: NS/CHP, 1991).

7. See Westerhoff, J. H., *Will Our Children Have Faith?* (Harrisburg, PA: Morehouse Publishing, 2012).

8. There are two more styles of faith in Westerhoff's scheme. As with the later stages of Fowler's scheme of faith development, they fall outside the remit of this book, but you can read about them in Westerhoff's writing.

9. Westerhoff, J. H., *Will Our Children Have Faith?*

10. Csinos, *Children's Ministry that Fits.*

Chapter 7

1. Hence the need for intergenerational worship. See chapter 11.

2. A good and readable book on this theory is Codrington and Grant-Marshall, *Mind the Gap.*

3. At the time of writing, the Christian unions in many universities have become even more fundamental than they were in my own student days. The type of faith that they seem to espouse is authoritarian and closed – very much the stage 3 of Fowler's scheme. This means that young people of faith who are attending to the questions and doubts of stage 4 are not able to find support in such a group and may give up their Christianity as a response.

4. I had such a group in my last church. We met once a month and talked about things that concerned them, and I encouraged them to bring ideas to this meeting to pass on to the adult church meetings. It was very good to hear their

ideas, which were often very much in line with adult thinking. We valued these young people as real members of the church, not just "the church in waiting".

Chapter 8

1. www.ofsted.gov.uk/resources/school-inspection-handbook.
2. Wolff Pritchard, G., *Offering the Gospel to Children* (Cambridge, MA: Cowley Publications, 1992).
3. The fact that many ministers feel that they are "not good with children" reinforces this way of sidelining children from the main body of the church during worship, and so from the day-to-day life of most of the worshippers.
4. See appendix 1 for a script of how to turn this story into an interactive telling. Also see www.assemblies.org.uk where it appears as a school assembly.
5. Berryman J. W., *Godly Play* (Minneapolis, MN: Augsburg Fortress, 1991)
6. Berryman J. W., *Teaching Godly Play* (Abingdon: Abingdon Press, 1995).
7. Please read the section in the appendix on Godly Play observed in schools for a summary of how important such a room can be for the learning that goes on.
8. A desert bag is a large drawstring bag containing a good quantity of sand. It can be opened out and forms an "instant desert" for telling the stories such as Abraham and Sarah. If you put the words "Godly Play desert bag" into a search engine, you will find lots of images.
9. See the script for "The Good Shepherd" in Berryman, J. W. and S. M. Stewart, *Young Children and Worship* (Louisville, KN: Westminster John Knox Press, 1989), p.85.
10. Lamont, R. "A comparison of the effect of storytelling on the spirituality of children aged nine and ten," MA (Pastoral Theology) dissertation, 2004, Anglia Polytechnic University (now Anglia Ruskin University).
11. Illustrating Winnicott's "third space", something Berryman speaks of in *Godly Play*.
12. Lamont, "A comparison of the effect of storytelling on the spirituality of children aged nine and ten".
13. Lamont, "A comparison of the effect of storytelling on the spirituality of children aged nine and ten".
14. Lamont, "A comparison of the effect of storytelling on the spirituality of children aged nine and ten".

Chapter 9

1. Sorea and Scârneci-Domnişoru, "Unorthodox Depictions of Divinity," p. 396.
2. White, K. J., *The Growth of Love* (Abingdon: Barnabas for Children, 2008).
3. https://www.childrenssociety.org.uk/what-we-do/resources-and-publications/the-good-childhood-report-2018 (April 2019), p. 12.
4. American psychologist Abraham Maslow stated something similar in his "hierarchy of needs" (1943), which you may have come across, or can find in the usual places if you are interested.
5. White, *The Growth of Love*, p. 31.

6. White, *The Growth of Love*, p. 32.

7. https://www.imdb.com/title/tt0107290/.

8. See any basic psychology book for explanation or https://en.wikipedia.org/wiki/File:Maslow%27s_hierarchy_of_needs.png#/media/File:Maslow%27s_hierarchy_of_needs.png.

9. Fox, M., *Original Blessing* (New York City: TarcherPerigee, 2000).

10. White, *The Growth of Love*, p. 150.

11. White, *The Growth of Love*, p. 154.

12. Peterson, E. H., *Christ Plays in Ten Thousand Places*, cited in Novelli, M., *Shaped by the Story* (Minneapolis, MN: Sparkhouse Press, 2013). Novelli's book on story is well worth investing in, as is Bettelheim, B., *The Uses of Enchantment* (London: Penguin, 1991).

13. Novelli, M., *Shaped by the Story*, p. 78.

14. Varley, S., *Badger's Parting Gifts* (New York City: HarperCollins, 1992).

15. White, *The Growth of Love*, p. 112.

16. White, *The Growth of Love*, p. 116.

17. White, *The Growth of Love*, p. 1.

18. Swimme, B., cited in Novelli, M., *Shaped by the Story*, p. 83.

19. Skolimowski, H., cited in Novelli, M., *Shaped by the* Story, p. 150.

20. Berryman J. W., *Godly Play* (Minneapolis, MN: Augsburg Fortress, 1991), p.1.

21. These sermons were published in the collection Lamont, R., *The God Who Leads Us On* (London: SPCK 2008). Out of print but available from the author.

22. Pridmore, J., *Playing with Icons* (The Center for the Theology of Childhood of the Godly Play Foundation, 2017), p. 67.

23. Eisenberg Sasso, S., *God In Between* (Woodstock, VT: Jewish Lights Publishing, 1998).

24. Berryman, *Godly Play*, p. 5.

25. Berryman, *Godly Play*, p. 6.

26. Winnicott, D. W., *Playing and Reality* (London: Tavistock, 1971).

27. Nye, R., *Children's Spirituality* (London: Church House Publishing, 2009).

28. Nye, *Children's Spirituality*, p. 52.

29. White, *The Growth of Love*, p. 104.

30. White, *The Growth of Love*, p. 105.

31. Richards, A and P. Privett, *Through the Eyes of a Child* (London: Church House Publishing, 2009), p. 105.

32. Richards and Privett, *Through the Eyes of a Child*, p. 107.

Chapter 10

1. My thanks go to Peter Wilson and the children of Old Bexley Church of England Primary School, and to Tony Linnett and the children of Hurst Primary School, for their input.

2. The turning away from fairy stories that has taken place over the last thirty years or so reflects this trend; people say that they don't want to expose their children to

such violent and grisly stories without realizing that one function of the grisly fairy story is to help children rehearse scenarios in the heads before they come across them in reality, and that these stories are actually very moral. For possibly the best book dealing with this, see Bettelheim, B., *The Uses of Enchantment: The Meaning and Importance of Fairy Tales* (London: Penguin, 1991).

3. Young, F., *Can These Dry Bones Live?* (Eugene, OR: Wipf and Stock Publishers, 2010).

4. For young children, *Badger's Parting Gifts* by Jane Varley is a delightful exploration of death. For older children, *Waterbugs and Dragonflies* by Doris Stickney (Cleveland, OH: The Pilgrim Press, 2004) is very helpful.

5. See www.assemblies.org.uk, a site run by SPCK, for examples of assemblies, with prayer/reflection for children of this age.

6. Defining God by saying what God is not is part of the Apophatic tradition.

7. Is this a flashback to watching *Telletubbies* (BBC/Wood Productions) when smaller, where the sun had a laughing cherubic toddler face superimposed?

8. This classic reasoning for God's existence is called the ontological argument.

9. I use the version in Berryman, J. W., *The Complete Guide to Godly Play, Vol 3* (Denver: CO, Living the Good News, 2002), or see www.godlyplay.org.

10. From Berryman, *The Complete Guide to Godly Play.*

Chapter 11

1. Sorea and Scârneci-Domnișoru, "Unorthodox depictions of divinity", p.390.

2. You will also get to know the local dogs and their owners.

3. I recommend https://www.canterburydiocese.org/childrenandschools/policies-and-guidance/ (last accessed December 2018).

4. See https://www.assemblies.org.uk/resources/advice-law/ for the nuts and bolts of what you can and cannot say and do.

5. As yet unpublished, but under the auspices of NICER (National Institute for Christian Education Research, Canterbury Christ Church University.

6. See https://www.godlyplay.uk/courses/3-day-accredited-core-training/.

7. See https://www.thykingdomcome.global/.

8. This was at a Shinto shrine in the town of Mishima.

9. For the complete pack, see https://www.canterburydiocese.org/advent-prayer-packs/.

10. See the Diocese of Gloucester website, https://www.gloucester.anglican.org/2017/experience-easter-resources/.

Chapter 12

1. Parochial Church Council. All Church of England churches are run by such a body, which, with the minister, has quite serious legal responsibilities.

2. Thanks to Murray Wilkinson for posing these two questions.

3. See www.godlyplay.uk.

4. https://www.youtube.com/watch?v=vbuq7w3ZDUQ.

5. See Hopewell, J. F., *Congregation* (Minneapolis, MN: Fortress Press, 1987) for an interesting account of how a congregation perceives and holds its own story.

6. See Savage, S. and E. Boyd-MacMillan, *The Human Face of Church* (Norwich: Canterbury Press, 2007) for a devastating analysis of the culture of "nice" within churches.

7. https://www.allsaintscanterbury.co.uk.

8. Years ago I read a story in the *Church Times* where a contributor visited a church whilst on holiday. At the end of the service, he was told that coffee was "just for the regulars."

9. Nye, *Children's Spirituality*.

10. Don't rely on extroverts being more enthusiastic about this sort of activity either – you get shy extroverts and confident introverts. See Cain, S., *Quiet* (London: Penguin, 2012).

11. See https://www.messychurch.org.uk/resource/messy-togetherness-being-intergenerational-messy-church.

Chapter 13

1. Revd Juliet Evans (previously Donnelly).

2. Assuming you are a Church of England church.

3. We had not been successful; the parish was a team, including an ecumenical church (Anglican/Roman Catholic/Baptist). If a parish is to proceed with Communion prior to confirmation, all the churches in the team must go forward together. Unfortunately, the Baptist element was not able to agree to this, so all of the churches in the team were prevented from going down this path. Yes, it was very frustrating!

4. I'm very grateful to my curate, Revd Juliet Donnelly, for her input to this course, which we devised together.

5. See appendix 1.

6. See appendix 2.

7. This is the age recommended by the General Synod. I have to admit to finding it fairly arbitrary; it's very small children who desperately put up their hands for communion at the rail. By the time they reach seven, they've learned that they won't get any. We agreed to two rising sevens in this cohort as both had older siblings and clearly wanted to be included. The decision was reached by balancing how much damage excluding these children would cause, in discussion with parents/carers. As much of the debate about giving children Communion at this age is to do with inclusion, we felt it would be doing more damage by saying no to these youngsters. They were all excellent students, and received with great joy and respect.

8. See Stewart, S. M. and J. W. Berryman, *Young Children and Worship* (Louisville, KN: Westminster John Knox Press, 1989), p. 85ff, or Berryman, J. W., *The Complete Guide to Godly Play, Vol 3*. Materials for Godly Play sessions can be bought from St Michael's Community Trust, 01603 746106, www.

bowthorpecommtrust@lineone.net. They take about six weeks to arrive. Or you can find a keen craftsperson to make these visual aids. Patterns are included in the books.

9. See Stewart and Berryman, *Young Children and Worship*, p. 189ff.

10. Berryman, J. W., *The Complete Guide to Godly Play*, Vol 4 (New York: Church Publishing, 2018), p. 81ff.

11. Don't forget your local diocesan or district office may well have Godly Play resources to lend out.

12. Berryman, J. W., *The Complete Guide to Godly Play*, Vol 2 (New York: Church Publishing, 2017) p. 41.

13. Berryman, *The Complete Guide to Godly Play*, Vol 2, p. 34.

14. Berryman, *The Complete Guide to Godly Play*, Vol 3, p. 97.

15. Stewart and Berryman, *Young Children and Worship*, p. 198.

16. Berryman, *Complete Guide to Godly Play*, Vol 4, p.106.

Appendix 1

1. Extended in 2019 for two more years.

2. Berryman *Godly Play*, p. 22.

3. Winnicott, D. W., *Playing and Reality* (London: Tavistock, 1971), p. 117.

4. The Story of the Holy Family features a baby Jesus with outstretched arms "waiting to give us a hug" and an adult Jesus with his arms out. Many interpret this as crucifixion, but the story states that the adult Jesus also "has his arms out, to give us a hug."

5. Pridmore, J., *Playing with Icons* (The Centre for the Theology of Childhood, 2017), p. 73.

6. Berryman, *Godly Play*.

7. Pridmore, *Playing with Icons*, p. 67.

BIBLIOGRAPHY

Axline, V., *Dibs: In Search of Self* (London: Penguin, 1990).

Bee, H. and D. Boyd, *The Developing Child* (London: Allyn & Bacon, 2006).

Bellous, J., D. Csinos and D. Peltomaki, *Spiritual Styles* (questionnaire/booklet) (Tall Pine Press, 2009).

Berryman, J. W., *Godly Play* (Minneapolis, MN: Augsburg Fortress, 1991).

Berryman, J. W., *The Complete Guide to Godly Play* (New York: Living the Good News, 2002).

Berryman, J. W., *The Complete Guide to Godly Play, Revised and Extended* (New York: Church Publishing, 2017).

Berryman J. W., *Teaching Godly Play* (Abingdon: Abingdon Press, 1995).

Best, E., *Mark: The Gospel as Story* (Edinburgh: T & T Clark, 1983).

Bettelheim, B., *The Uses of Enchantment* (London: Penguin, 1991).

Cain, S., *Quiet* (London: Penguin, 2012).

Cavalletti, S., *The Religious Potential of the Child* (New York: Paulist Press, 1979).

Codrington, G. and S. Grant-Marshall, *Mind the Gap* (London: Fig Tree, 2011).

Coggins, R. J. and J. L. Houlden, *A Dictionary of Biblical Interpretation* (London/Philadelphia: SCM/TPI, 1990).

Coles, R., *The Spiritual Life of Children* (Boston, MS: Houghton Mifflin, 1990).

Copsey, K., *From the Ground Up* (Oxford: Barnabas, 2005).

Csinos, D., *Children's Ministry that Fits* (Eugene, OR: Wipf and Stock, 2011).

Erikson, E. H., *Childhood and Society* (London: Vintage, 1995).

Fowler, J. W., *Faith Development and Pastoral Care* (Philadelphia: Fortress, 1987).

Fowler, J. W., *Stages of Faith* (San Francisco: Harper Collins, 1995).

Fowler, J. W., K. Nipkow and F. Schweitzer, *Stages of Faith and Religious Development* (Philadelphia: Fortress, 1987).

General Synod Board of Education, *Children in the Way* (London: NS/CHP, 1991).

General Synod Board of Education, *All God's Children?* (London: NS/CHP, 1991).

General Synod Board of Education, *How Faith Grows* (London: NS/CHP, 1991).

Goldingay, J., *After Eating the Apricot* (Cumbria: Solway, 1996).

Hay, D., *Something There* (London: DLT, 2006).

Hay, D. and R. Nye, *The Spirit of the Child* (London: Fount, 1998).

Hopewell, J. F., *Congregation: Stories and Structures* (Minneapolis, MN: Augsburg Fortress, 1987).

Kirkpatrick, L. A. and P. R. Shaver, "Attachment theory and religion; Childhood attachments, religious beliefs and conversion," *Journal for the Scientific Study of Religion*, 29, 3: 315-34, 1992.

Lamont, R., "A comparison of the effect of storytelling on the spirituality of children aged nine and ten," MA (Pastoral Theology) dissertation, 2004, Anglia Polytechnic University (now Anglia Ruskin University).

Loder, J., *The Transforming Moment* (Colorado Springs, CO: Helmers and Howard, 1989).

Miller-McLemore, B., *Let the Children Come* (San Francisco: Jossey-Bass, 2003).

Novelli, M., *Shaped by the Story* (Minneapolis, MN: Sparkhouse Press, 2013).

Nye, R., *Children's Spirituality* (London: Church House Publishing, 2009).

Pollerman, S., *Stories, Stories Everywhere* (Oxford: Barnabas, 2001).

Pridmore, J., *Playing with Icons: The Spirituality of Recalled Childhood* (The Center for the Theology of Childhood of the Godly Play Foundation, Pescola, FL, 2017).

Rayner, E., A. Joyce, J. Rose, M. Twyman and C. Clulow, *Human Development* (Abingdon: Routledge, 2005).

Reed, B., *The Dynamics of Religion* (London: DLT, 1978).

Richards, A. and P. Privett, *Through the Eyes of a Child* (London: Church House Publishing, 2009).

Rizzuto, A-M., *The Birth of the Living God* (Chicago: University of Chicago Press, 1979).

Roberto, J., *Faith Formation with a New Generation* (Cheshire: Lifelong Faith Publications, 2018).

Savage, S. and E. Boyd-MacMillan, *The Human Face of Church* (Norwich: Canterbury Press, 2007).

Schaffer H. R., *The Child's Entry into a Social World* (London: Academic Press, 1984).

Slee, N., "Parable Teaching: Exploring new worlds," *British Journal of Religious Education*, 5, 1983.

Sorea, D. and F. Scârneci-Domnişoru, "Unorthodox Depictions of Divinity: Romanian children's drawings of Him, Her or It," *The International Journal of Children's Spirituality*, Vol 23, 4, 2018.

Stewart, S. M. and J. W. Berryman, *Young Children and Worship* (Louisville, KN: Westminster John Knox Press, 1989).

Tamminen, K., *Religious Development in Childhood and Youth* (Helsinki: Suomalainen Tiedeakatemia, 1991).

Walker, A., *Telling the Story* (London: SPCK, 1996).

Watts, F., R. Nye and S. Savage, *Psychology for Christian Ministry* (Abingdon: Routledge, 2002).

Westerhoff, J., *Will Our Children Have Faith?* (Harrisburg, PA: Morehouse Publishing, 2012).

White, K. J., *The Growth of Love* (Abingdon: Barnabas for Children, 2008).

Winnicott, D. W., *Playing and Reality* (London: Tavistock, 1971).

Withers, M., *Mission-Shaped Children* (London: Church House Publishing, 2006).

Wolff Pritchard, G., *Offering the Gospel to Children* (Cambridge, MA: Cowley Publications, 1992).

Wood, D., *How Children Think and Learn* (Oxford: Blackwell, 1998).

Yust, K. M., *Real Kids Real Faith* (San Francisco: Jossey-Bass, 2004)

INDEX